Hattie was my saviour! I had a young baby that hadn't slept longer than 3-hour stretches for months. I was beyond broken and a shadow of my former self. With sound logical advice and a boat load of experience, she not only got my baby sleeping through within a couple of days but gave me back my sanity. Full of fairy dust, her book contains the same sound, sage advice. If it helps you as much as she helped me then this is worth its weight in gold!
—Nikki Earthrowl

Expectant parents: you NEED this incredible book to guide you through the first 12 weeks! Hattie's honest and authoritative approach is just what you want as you navigate the minefield of parenthood. All of your questions (and trust me there will be lots) will be answered.
—TS, Clapham

Having a baby is the probably the biggest emotional rollercoaster life can throw at you. Trust me: you need this book to get you through the first 12 weeks. Everyone has an opinion on how to look after a newborn but if you've read Hattie's informative book you will be prepared for every step!
—Fran Snowball

Hattie's book comes from decades of hands-on experience with newborns and new parents. If you read it, you will get through the first 12 weeks in style and with a smile on your face. Now that's saying something.

—First time mum, London

The information Hattie gave me about awake/sleep times, swaddling, and how to help to help my baby learn to self-settle was just life changing! Every new mum needs to brace themselves for the feelings of overwhelm. Be reassured that everything is phase, and phases pass. The varied and conflicting advice/opinions out there will make your head spin, so Hattie's book is a great place to start for some sensible, fact-based advice.

—Second time mum, Balham

I struggled through the first few months with my new baby. She wouldn't sleep anywhere but on me and seemed to cry all the time. We were drowning until we found Hattie. Her warm smile, unwavering patience and no-nonsense tried-and-tested advice completely transformed our lives — pretty much overnight. A fairy Godmother and modern-day Mary Poppins rolled into one. This book will change your life!

—Monique Borsi

The First 12 Weeks with a New Baby

(The WTF Happens Now? Guide)

Hattie Weeks

postnatal coaching
with Hattie Weeks

www.hattieweeks.com

Dirty Nappy Publishing™

Wimbledon, England

www.hattieweeks.com

2 3 4 5 6 7 8 9 10

First edition 2020

Printed in the United Kingdom

ISBN: 978-1-5272-6091-7

TABLE OF CONTENTS

ACKNOWLEDGEMENTS

Some writers hide this page right at the back of their books, but I feel that thanks are necessary first and foremost.

There were many of my clients who said, "You should write a book". But there were some who really, really pushed me to do it, and for that I am grateful.

So, I'd like to thank:

My husband Brent for so patiently unravelling my endless struggles with technology and for his eternal belief in me.

And a few of my ex clients:

Mummy Melissa: It was you who suggested I begin coaching all those years ago and I am so grateful that I listened.

Mummy Fran: For your patience and support as a coach during the early stages of getting words out of my head and onto paper.

Mummy Nikki: for hauling one of the early drafts halfway

round the world on your holiday so that you could read it and give me feedback as a mum.

Mummy Monique: for your constant encouragement and enthusiasm in cheering me forward with it and for taking the time to help me get to grips with social media a little.

Mummy Becca & Baby George (aka "Little Shit"): who made me laugh 'til I wept at every session and showed me that it is positively therapeutic to fit the F-word into each and every sentence when you become a new mother!

INTRODUCTION

"IF YOU CAN WRIGGLE YOUR WAY THROUGH THIS BOOK BEFORE
YOU HAVE YOUR BABY, YOU WILL BE WELL ARMED WITH SENSIBLE,
RELIABLE AND CONSISTENT KNOWLEDGE WITH WHICH TO
TAKE THAT LEAP INTO PARENTHOOD".

O K. Straight off the bat for my opener: There is no such thing as the perfect parent!

And quite frankly, if such a creature existed, they would probably be shunned and despised by the vast population of ordinary, imperfect parents! The ones who are just muddling through. The sleep deprived mothers who are doing the best they can to get to the end of every day with both their child and their own sanity intact.

This book is not about me telling you how you bring up your children. It's about passing forward some of my experience with newborns and help you to *get through* the first three months of life as parents in one piece.

As newbies, you will have opinions and theories from others thrust upon you until you want to time-travel back into the Stone

Age. Apparently, this is when they all knew how to do things so much better than us.

Stone Age Mums quite possibly breast fed on demand until their offspring could hunt, kill, peel and cook a mammoth independently; a Free Range, Organic Mammoth, naturally!

They never totally lost their shit when their mate was late back from the watering hole, they slept peacefully round the campfire in the cave and their babies were contented little bundles of joy. They were a shining example of how nature intended people to bring up children and they all lived happily ever after.

Meh! I don't think so. Neither did a very erudite and eloquent anthropologist whom I coached over his first three months as a new dad a few months ago.

Listening to some of his accounts about how different cultures raise their children would make your average Yummy Mummy's freshly highlighted hair stand on end.

He went on to explain, "Modern western parents are under the impression that in tribal villages, babies are carried round with the mother all day long, fed on demand and that they barely cry and certainly never have "witching hours" in the evenings. It's just a well pedalled bit of propaganda and it should be reassuring to learn that their babies are as hellish in the evenings as some of ours."

In Mongolia, babies were traditionally bundled up in blankets, snug and tight. This was to make them easier to deal with when riding around on horses. Their babies learned social skills by simply watching and imitating. They were scolded or physically punished for any naughty behaviour. Their role within the tribe was established by the age of 5-6 years, often sleeping outside overnight while looking after herds of sheep or goats. They learned to ride at about the same time as they did to walk.

That said, readers of this book are very unlikely to live deep in the Amazonian jungles, nor cantering around on a horse in Mongolia or anywhere much further afield than Penzance, frankly. Nor will they be in possession of baby-journals handed down through generations of Stone Age Ancestors, on which to base any credible arguments.

We live in houses and have buggies (now rather grandly referred to as, erm, "Travel Systems" by snooty shop assistants in certain department stores), cots and cribs into which we can safely insert our little blessings whilst we get on with our days. There they can sleep soundly, well away from pterodactyls, tarantulas, goat-stealing eagles and suchlike.

If you are not yet a parent, then please brace yourself. Somewhere out there is a tidal wave of judgement, conflicting opinion, wild theories and misinformation and it is heading your way. If you can wriggle your way through this book before you have your baby, you will be well armed with sensible, reliable and consistent knowledge with which to take that leap into parenthood.

Please read this book from one end to the other, rather than skipping back and forth. There is a method to the books' construction, and the aim is to feed you the information in time-relevant sections. When you follow a recipe, you don't start with only half the ingredients and midway through the method — so please try not to do that with my book. It took a lot of time and effort to extrapolate 24 years' worth of knowledge from my mind and dump it onto paper! It took even more work to formulate a book that a parent can follow without getting lost in the pages.

WHO IS HATTIE WEEKS ANYWAY?

"... I HAVE BEEN ABLE TO ACCUMULATE A WEALTH OF EXPERIENCE AND KNOWLEDGE. IN TURN, THIS HAS HELPED ME COACH THOUSANDS OF MUMS, BUILDING THEIR CONFIDENCE WHILE GETTING BACK TO BASICS."

I don't know how it feels to push something the size of a Christmas Turkey out of my birth canal. Nor have I known the searing love some mothers feel when they first clap eyes on their child. But by GOD I understand how a newborn baby's cry can make you feel as though someone has wrapped barbed wire around your heart … and then pulled it out through your chest.

I am an aunt four times over, and my heart has had the barbed wire treatment many times.

I have a smashing niece. Occasionally I was allowed to babysit when she was very tiny. She cried so hard as I left her room at bedtime that I thought my heart might burst, so I spent the entire evening lying on the floor beside the cot, holding her little hand through the bars until she fell asleep. She had made me her slave within about two minutes.

Not being the strictest babysitter back then, her tremulous cry rendered me incapable of rational thought. I was putty in her hands and she knew it. As a result, I spent many evenings just lying on the floor as we looked lovingly at each other through the cot bars. I lost the battle completely.

Now an adult in her thirties, we have a great relationship, and our "babysitting" stories include her pouring my glass of wine into the fish tank and her peeing in a shoe cupboard when I took just a teeny bit too long to "find" her when playing Hide & Seek.

If she reads this introduction, especially the bit about the shoe cupboard, she will probably never speak to me again. Love you Jen!

I also have three equally loved nephews. Triplets. Sean, Jack & Luke.

As an end result of *their* arrival a few years after my niece, I changed career and began working with newborns. That was twenty-four years ago, and although no one will ever believe me, as I write this sentence it was actually 24 years ago *yesterday* that the dramas began.

My brother's wife had announced her pregnancy over champagne and hugs at Christmas. A "big fat baby" was expected the following August.

Having just accepted a job in Africa, working as a professional Dive Guide aboard a luxury yacht, I was due to start the following September. This job demanded a two-month trial period which involved cruising around the Indian Ocean, taking people diving. I know … a shit job, right? — yeah! But someone had to do it. I flew out in January to begin my trial and was living the dream.

After receiving an overseas call from my brother informing me that they had had their first scan, and that my Aunty Hattie status had been significantly upgraded, I was stunned to find I was now destined to become an aunty, Aunty, AUNTY Hattie.

I returned to the UK in April, finding myself a seasonal job in Devon so that I could be around when the babies were due later that summer. A much colder, wetter and far less glamorous job, working as one of three permanent crew members aboard a magnificent Edwardian schooner, based in Salcombe, Devon. For those of you who don't know much about boats, that's a very big yacht with lots and lots of sails!

Having enjoyed some brisk, chilly spring sailing, I was looking forward to some warmer days on deck in the summer months when, dramatically, my appendicitis kicked off. It was early July, Day 2 of a three-week charter trip, halfway across the Irish Sea. I had worked on the boat for only three months.

An urgent removal from the yacht was followed by rather swift and brutal appendectomy, carried out in a strange geriatric hospital in southern Ireland. Three weeks later I was discharged and temporarily adopted by the owners of a local Yacht Marina, allowing me to stay with them until I was fit enough to fly home; perhaps this was the upside of working aboard a rather famous vessel.

Unfortunately, within 24 hours I had a temperature of 105° and was very poorly indeed. I was rushed to Cork University Hospital in the back of an ambulance for three blood transfusions. After a further three weeks of recovery, I was flown back to the UK where I convalesced at my parents' home.

By crashing into this world within days of this event, my nephews Sean, Jack & Luke altered the trajectory of my working life. Within the space of a year, I was immersed in the world of poo, howling babies and new parenthood. I'm not sure I have entirely forgiven them, even now.

Sadly, the medical complications following my operation left me physically unable to cope with the rigorous demands of life aboard such a sailing vessel. I was also unable to return to diving for at least six months. I had to kiss goodbye to my African adventure and was heartbroken. I was also hideously bad company to have around as a result.

My mother diplomatically suggested I help out with my new nephews. For someone who worked as a dive guide in a tropical paradise, this proposal was greeted with a slack-jawed silence from my end. You've GOT to be kidding me! Babies? Yuck! Noisy, ungrateful, smelly little things. I was not a baby person in any way, shape or form. Was she MAD?

Regardless, and with steely determination on my mother's part, I was firmly herded down to Devon where I was able to spend several months helping my brother, sister-in-law and the three new boys, born only days before I was teetering on the brink of an appendectomy on board a yacht in the middle of the Irish Sea!

Baptism by fire doesn't even scratch the surface. How they survived is beyond me, and that's just the parents! But survive they did. We all did.

The three little lads were resilient, forgiving my every mistake. Eventually, they greeted me with smiles and giggles when I arrived every morning, remaining enduringly patient with my clumsiness and impatience. I wrestled with nappy changes, bathing and dressing/undressing them — which, for the record, was like trying to insert an angry octopus into a condom. They fought me every inch of the way but eventually I got the measure of them.

Nothing really prepares you for the impact of a new baby. *Absolutely* nothing prepares you for the arrival of three of the little buggers. I learnt on the job and you will too. My legendary sister-in-law and my little brother set their jaws firm, took a deep breath, waded into battle with grit, strength and just got the job done.

I am forever in their debt and cannot begin to fathom how much teamwork it took to finally raise three fine young men under such stress. A perfect blend of steel and love, the like of which I have never seen before or since.

I returned to London several months after the boys were born and started working as a Maternity Nanny, offering 24-hour support to new parents for six out of seven days per week. For a while, I even managed to strike a balance between helping mums for a few months and then disappearing to exotic places to dive, so it worked out rather well.

Several years later, I began to realise that, unless a mother is bottle feeding her baby, my presence overnight was somewhat excess to requirements. I began taking daytime maternity bookings and completed a Birth & Postnatal Doula course. I furiously took notes about every baby with whom I worked, observing their body language, their sounds, their ups and downs until I began to see a pattern.

It was based on these experiences that I began to really understand how babies function, what they can and can't cope with, and when to introduce different structures to their days. New babies need to sleep for huge amounts of time, but often don't because they are not understood yet. Once this communication between parent and baby is better explained, a new level of calm can be found and, whilst still often a tiring and frustrating period, the newborn weeks become more manageable.

It was a client of mine who suggested that I offer postnatal coaching to new mums and I've not looked back. Well, perhaps a little wistfully, dreaming about on which island paradise I might have ended up as a Dive Guide, had the universe not concocted its little Plan B.

So, in a rather large nutshell, that is how I came to be Hattie Weeks, the Postnatal Coach.

One doesn't have to have physically given birth to learn how these little people function, understand their needs and wants, or how to best help them transition into the world.

You decide who you are and how you want to parent. How you were raised may have a significant impact on your choices. I was bought up by parents who loved and encouraged me. They were firm and fair. They did not try to be my best friend and I knew exactly where my boundaries lay. That made me feel safe and loved.

When they died only 15 months apart, I knew that the hole they left in my life would never, ever be filled. I adored them both and had the bitter-sweet privilege of being with them both in the weeks and then minutes before they left us. They saw me come into this life, so there was a comfort in being able to give them a kiss and see them set off to their next one.

There are divided opinions about the age at which you should start a newborn on a routine, if at all — and people can be quite aggressive and vocal with their views.

By watching the little people in my care and learning to interpret what they were trying to tell me, I have been able to accumulate a wealth of experience and knowledge. In turn, this has helped me coach thousands of mums, building their confidence while getting back to basics.

Perhaps by harmonising with a baby's natural feeding patterns and sleep cycles, we can help them to establish good habits at an early stage, which in turn makes for a much less stressful journey for all concerned.

Mothers should be allowed to feel instinctive. They should not be a lonely and relentlessly critiqued group. Nor should babies be treated like mythical creatures that need to be prodded, medicated, analysed and labelled every day of their young lives.

Babies don't often need to be "fixed". They need to be understood, translated and allowed to grow and develop as nature intended, without parents feeling yet more pressure to meet the demands of the latest fad or fashion of parenting.

How you raise your children may replicate your own upbringing. Yet, if all generations did just that, many parents would still be spanking a naughty two-year-old or leaving infants to cry in their pram in the garden for an hour without responding.

It is worth bearing in mind that with many aspects of newborn care, it is merely a case of what works for you and your baby. Some families thrive on the predictability of a routine and strive to get one established as soon as possible. Others are more laid back and prefer to just take each hour as it comes.

This makes being a new mum even more confusing. I often remind people that *The Contented Little Baby Book, The Baby Whisperer* and other such baby bibles are written as a guide, not an instruction manual to be followed to the letter. Some of my friends have used several different reference books and have found that does the trick. They pluck what they feel relevant, leaving the rest for others.

You may find some wisdom amongst my words. Equally you may feel that some of it just doesn't work for you. That is fine. If you manage to unearth some snippets which are helpful, it may help you transition from your pre-baby life to your new one as a parent, with just a little more knowledge than you had before.

When building a routine, it's much like learning to drive a car or work your way up to fitness perfection. You don't thunder off down the motorway at 70mph minutes after you get behind the wheel, nor do you replace the flabs with abs within a week of joining a gym. You start slowly and work your way up.

Now, please read on and I will try to walk you through things in little steps. Baby steps. This does not culminate in an exam and you are not cramming for a degree. So just dip into this book and know that it has been written with love and humour.

I hope it will help you through the first twelve weeks. I want to show you that the soft-focused, squeaky-clean, heart-meltingly beautiful images on social media, depicting the early weeks are chasms away from the reality. That little bit of knowledge will serve to make you feel a whole lot better about the vortex into which you are about to hurl yourself.

The layout in these pages is intended to prepare you in stages.

This should enable you see what to expect ahead of time. It will help you understand a little better how to cope when you are in the thick of it, offer tips and suggestions to coach you over the tough times, lighten the mood and make you laugh along the way.

Like good girl scouts, I'm all about being prepared. Assuming you approach this book as it was intended, you will thumb through the pages and tick boxes to make sure you are One Step Ahead from now. If you don't, you will have to muddle through, manage a little bit of catch-up reading and then join the party in a few pages.

I will refer to the baby throughout this book as a "he" for ease of editing, so baby girls please excuse me.

LEARNING IN CHUNKS

"...PLEASE TRY TO FOCUS ON READING THROUGH
THIS BOOK PAGE BY PAGE".

HOW TO APPROACH THIS BOOK

It may be tempting to simply flick through the following pages until you land in a section that you feel is relevant to the moment, or the crisis, or the conundrum in which you currently find yourselves. But please try to focus on reading through this book page by page.

As you work from the start of the book, I aim to cover topics with which you will need to familiarise yourself over the first two weeks following the birth, as well as a few months of planning before the baby arrives.

I am not big on humour during some of the early chapters, because, quite frankly, most of it is pretty serious stuff and not to be taken lightly.

Once I have talked you through the first week or two, then I will start to relax a little and my rather offbeat humour will begin to creep into the text. After a couple of weeks, you may have experienced some or all of the early days blips and be in a position to start taking on board a little daily guidance.

I'm not going to bombard you with endless testimonials either. Frankly, if it were me, I couldn't be less interested in hearing about what someone else's little Romulus or Millicent's problems were, nor how the author solved them. I don't mean that unkindly, but it just highlights the current trend of assuming that whatever works for Romulus and Millicent will work for your own baby, which it probably won't; and if it doesn't you will feel like you are failing, which you are not!

CHAPTER 1

REALITY STRIKES

"YOU WILL YEARN FOR SOMEONE TO TELL YOU WITH PINPOINT
ACCURACY THAT SUCH-AND-SUCH A METHOD WILL GUARANTEE
A CERTAIN OUTCOME. THERE ARE NO SUCH PLATITUDES
IN THE WORLD OF BABIES."

Whatever journey you have been on thus far, you are now only weeks away from the most unpredictable and challenging leg yet.

Over the next twelve weeks you will be playing the parenting equivalent of Blind Man's Buff. My family played this at Christmas when we were young children, and we loved it.

In those days, TV had two channels and we weren't allowed to watch either of them! Broadcasting didn't start until gone 6pm, you see. By that time, we had been fed, bathed and were being treated to another story from "Strewelpeter, Cautionary Tales for Young Children", before being tucked up in bed. We were hardcore in those days.

The stories, especially when my father read them, both thrilled and slightly scared us in equal measure as he pretended to be the characters in the book, and we giggled and squealed our way under the covers. It would infuriate my mother, who was anxious that we were kept calm before bedtime. Some things never change!

For those of you who have not been subjected to post-Christmas Lunch parlour games, this is how Blind Man's Buff works. You are chosen as "It"; you are then blindfolded and repeatedly spun around until giddy and disorientated.

Wait, wait! This really *is* a book about babies so you can stop checking the front cover.

Work with me here.

Where was I? ... Blind Man's Buff, blindfolded, spun ... OK yes ... you are spun around repeatedly until, once completely dizzy and confused, you are released. Your friends scatter around the room, giggling and squealing as they try to avoid you. It is your task to catch them.

You have to explore the room, head tilted back (never understood why people do that — I mean it's not like we have two spare eyeballs up our nostrils is it?), arms failing in front of you in pursuit of your prey.

Every time you catch someone, they are "out". You score a point. In the process you blunder around the room, falling into chairs or cracking your shins on coffee tables. Your friends laugh and run away. Actually, now that I am committing my childhood memories to paper, it calls my family's idea of Christmas fun into question. Still, it was more fun than most modern Christmas TV programmes.

Anyhoo, in this parenting parallel you are the blind one and the friends are the solutions to problems you will encounter along the way. Evasive, transient and infuriatingly difficult to find.

Armed with the information given to you by your antenatal class, if you attended one at all, you'll plunge into life with your new baby, then realise that you honestly don't have a clue what you are doing. Each day will see you experiencing euphoria and despair, confusion and clarity, overwhelm and even underwhelm.

Take comfort from the fact that all new parents travel a similar route as they grope their way through the highs and lows of becoming first-timers.

Rather than presenting you with an unconquerable heap of information to wade through, I hope that this book will simply offer you pieces to chew on as you Blind-Man's-Buff your way to feeling slightly more empowered and confident than you did on your first day at home.

I am going to share with you little morsels gleaned from my time working with over 6,000 tiny people over the past 24 years, so that everything seems a little less daunting and a little more do-able on a week by week basis.

I have spent time with more babies aged 0-12 weeks than anyone I know, so as a result I feel that I have served my time and may have something fresh to offer to first time parents by way of guidance.

My clients, past and present (and future, if they are crazy enough to keep having more) have nagged me for many years about doing a book, so eventually I have decided to give it a go.

They all told me to "keep it real and write it as you would speak it".

"Most of all", they begged, "don't give the impression that the early weeks with a newborn are a misty-eyed trip down Buttercup Lane", as frequently portrayed on social media.

Don't imagine that your mornings will be, hmm … spent having freshly prepped fruit salad with organic yoghurt and a steaming cup of decaf on your balcony, lazily leafing through a copy of "My Beautiful House" magazine; meanwhile your precious infant lies sleeping peacefully in their laced-bedecked crib in their perfect, tidy, white nursery. It almost certainly won't' be like that, unless you have 24/7 cover from several dedicated career maternity nurses, a private chef, a cleaner, a chauffeur, a housekeeper and PA back there too.

Parents who tackle the implementing of routines with grit and unwavering determination may well coax their children to drop a night feed earlier than I suggest in this book.

That's wonderful for them. But it's just a little galling for new parents to hear that boast when they are not yet getting a full eight hours, when their baby still needs feeding twice nightly at three or four months of age, perhaps having been plagued with reflux, milk intolerances or cow's milk protein allergy (CPMA).

When looking for a definitive answer to questions, you'll become familiar with the greys. Not black. Not white. But grey.

You will yearn for someone to tell you with pinpoint accuracy that such-and-such a method will guarantee a certain outcome. There are no such platitudes in the world of babies. They are infuriatingly random little buggers and certainly they are not that keen on following the rules of grown-ups for a while.

So, without further fluffing about, let's approach things in a logical timeline, rather than rushing straight to the utopia: a baby who sleeps for 12 hours a night. That is a way off yet, so as a famously smug singing-nanny once warbled, "Let's start at the very beginning".

CHAPTER 2

GET THE CREDIT CARDS READY

"WE WANT TO COVER ALL WE CAN TO AVOID THE MASSIVE TEMPER TANTRUMS THAT MAY ENSUE ON YOUR HOMECOMING DAY".

WHAT WILL I NEED TO BUY?

For many, the first few months of pregnancy is all about how lovely it is to be nurturing this little life inside them. They are mentally decorating the nursery and dreaming of a life with their new baby, when it is little more than a lentil in size. For others perhaps it's a clandestine shopping trip on-line, wondering how much you can get away with ordering from The White Company or a chi-chi Parisian baby concierge before your (or your husband's/ partner's) credit card melts.

For some parents-to-be it has been a long, emotional and profoundly challenging time, perhaps blighted with interminable morning sickness, rounds of IVF and certainly no walk in the park.

Some may have previously lost a little soul along the way and now feel reluctant, or even scared, to allow themselves to be so excited the second or even third time they find they are pregnant.

So, let's not assume that everyone has their nursery all set up, the crib smothered in billowing layers of broderie anglaise or their cupboards crammed with every product that ever filled the stands at the London Baby Show.

Instead, I will be bold enough to presume that you have nothing other than your steadily growing bump, and a great sense of bewilderment creeping up on you.

I envisage you sitting back, like a member of the audience eagerly awaiting a performance of "The Woman in Black". Awash with the stories passed down by *Other Parents* who have been there before you, knowing that it's going to be brilliant yet scary. But *Other Parents* didn't want to spoil the ending, so you wait, quivering with anticipation, for the story to unfold.

"Righty ho!", she says, smiling sweetly.

Then, in a Mary Poppinsy kind of way, feet firmly planted at the ten-to-two position, while straightening her bun and smoothing down her starched, white apron, "Let's look at your house to start with."

I don't mean in a stalker-ish kind of way, furtively dressed in a grey raincoat, from the other side of the street in a parked car, but from a practical and pragmatic approach.

We want to cover all we can to avoid the massive temper tantrums that may ensue on your Homecoming Day.

For example, you forgot to factor in that you don't actually *have* a bath in your bathroom (and babies *properly* dislike power showers!), or that you live on the 5th floor of a building with no lift and are having a C-section delivery.

It is well worth jumping on to your local Mummy Facebook Page and checking out if some of the more expensive/short lifespan items are up for sale. Things like baby baths, cribs or Moses Baskets, Bouncy Chairs and Activity Mats etc. are only used for a small window of time compared to buggies and car seats, so you could certainly save a few quid by buying second-hand where possible.

As a mum-to-be you are a salesperson's dream come true and, before you know it, you will have a carload of kit costing £1,000 that you could have snapped up for £100 elsewhere.

You can buy a brand new mattress and fitted sheets for cots and cribs, replace covers for bouncy chairs, fling an activity mat in the washing machine; a baby bath can be given a swift wash down with some anti-bacterial spray to make it perfectly acceptable in your own home. As most clothing ends up covered in poo, pee or puke sooner or later in the first few months, you may as well do a bumper shop for baby-grows at a cheaper supermarket rather than buying hand-knitted works of art which will get ruined.

Certainly, it is worth putting out a call to any friends or relatives who have older children to see what they still have stashed away in their lofts or cupboards. In the bedlam that is the first few years with children, they may not have flogged off their stuff and quite possibly would be really grateful to get rid of the clobber (to make room for more clobber!) and save themselves a trip to the charity shop further down the line. A couple of bottles of nice wine in exchange for a mini house clearance seems a fair barter to me.

As a first-time mum-to-be, it's always fun mooching around baby shops and nursery departments as you buy all your brand-new kit. But before you head off to any Baby Shows or launch into what is undoubtedly going to be a long and happy Clickfest Romance on Amazon over the next few months, let's examine a few practical considerations, some of which may influence your buying decisions.

BABY'S NEW HOME

What? No, no, nooooo … No!

It *used* to be yours, but trust me, the baby will totally own it within a matter of days. Use this checklist to highlight any pitfalls you may have missed.

Access Considerations:
- Does your home have steps up from street level?
  Can a buggy rest safely on top step area without running away from you (while you wrestle with the keys … in the rain … and the baby shrieks at you … and you haven't had more than 3 hours of sleep since last Wednesday)?
- Does the house/flat have steps down from street level?
  Can you manhandle a buggy down the steps?
- Can you store a buggy just inside the front door area?
- If you live on a higher floor, is there a lift and will it accommodate your buggy?

- How many bedrooms are there?
  If two or more, can one be dedicated as a nursery?
- How close is your bedroom to the nursery? You'll need to think about signal efficiency for a baby monitor if on a separate floor.
- Is there a bathroom on the same floor as the nursery?
- Do you only have a shower room? (Might need a baby bath on a stand if that's the case)
- Do you have a bath with integrated shower area?
  If yes, does bath have a glass shower screen, and if so, does it open outwards?
- Is there enough room to lift baby out of bath onto a mat/ towel on the floor?
- How wide is the entrance area inside the front door?
  If considerably wider than the buggy, you should be fine.
- If you live in a flat, how wide is the space just inside the front door?
  If less than 1m wider than the buggy, things could be awkward.
- How high is the threshold in through the front door?
  Check this by walking like a flamingo. If you live in Cornwall or have never seen a flamingo, then think heron. Then get your partner to measure the height of your raised foot. Then you can stop being a flamingo … or a heron.
- Consider whether you could safely manoeuvre buggy & baby over that height?
- Could you do the same with a 3-month-old hippo and two bags of coal in the buggy? Think ahead: Babies get big-

ger. And *much* heavier. And there will be shopping. Lots of shopping!

Storage Considerations:
- Where can you store a buggy with wet/muddy wheels once inside the door?
- Is there a caretaker's area or cupboard you can borrow for a while?
- Are you allowed to store your buggy in a communal hallway?
- How far from your front door is your car garaged/parked? *You may be able to store your buggy in the boot of the car sometimes.*
- If you have a car, could you safely leave the buggy in the boot and just use a car seat for going in and out?
- If you have a portable car seat, could you transport the baby to and from the house in that? *If you don't have a car, you'll need a car seat to come home from hospital by taxi. It's the law. (Some of the more upmarket taxi companies in London can provide a car seat if you ask in advance).*
- Do you have pets who also need to fit into the car? Can you fit pet and buggy in the back?
- Will you have to get out of the house to walk a dog at the same time as getting out with the baby?
- Do you need to buy a larger car now?

Additional considerations for the Country Life:

- If you have a car, how far is it kept from the house? Think about rain, snow and darkness.
- Can you stash a buggy in a shed or lean-to?
- Are you happy wheeling a mud-slathered buggy through your front door?
- Can you fit the buggy and yourself into a hallway at the same time?
- Can you manage to fit baby, buggy and pet into the same vehicles for walks?
- Do you have a gravel driveway (buggies & gravel are not a good match)?

NEW BABY'S SHOPPING LIST

NAPPIES

The leakage rating of a nappy generally boils down to the size of your new baby's little bum. A chubby bum fills the inner nappy lining better, hence less sideways squirt risk.

A newborn may not have much of a bottom for a couple of weeks and accidents may happen from time to time, so it could be a case of trying out a few brands till you find one that works for them. As baby chubs up a bit, you can swap between brands until you settle on one that suits you. Sorry, one that suits your *baby*! (Otherwise that's just a bit weird!)

👶 REUSABLE NAPPIES

Nifty little pouches which have re-usable linings. You are going to be washing everything else covered in pee, puke and poo for the foreseeable future, so do our poor old planet a favour and consider Eco Friendly options, or you may see images of Greta Thunberg coming to haunt you in the poo patterns!

There are hundreds of makes now available and this should go some way to reducing the carbon footprint left by generations of the toxic nappy landfill, created over the past 30 years.

Some areas offer a Collect-Wash-Return service for reusable nappy liners.

👶 DISPOSABLE NAPPY SACKS

Again, you will find bio-degradable ones in the supermarkets/chemists next to the nappy area.

👶 NAPPY DISPOSAL UNIT

A compact bin which wraps and holds dirty nappies rather like a string of sausages. Once full, the string is simply cut free, tied up and the whole lot can be put in the bin. No mess, no smell and idiot proof. Useful if space is limited in the nursery.

👶 12 COTTON MUSLINS: 60CM X 60CM

To be used for wiping, shoulder-covering and general mopping up of baby goop.

🧍 **4 BIG BAGS OF LARGE COTTON WOOL BALLS**

The ones they try to sell you in the "baby" departments are more expensive and smaller and no use unless your baby has a head the size of a tennis ball. The larger ones are man enough for the job and best for cleaning their eyes and around their faces.

🧍 **4 PACKS OF THE PLEATED COTTON WOOL**

Poos can cover acres, so cotton wool balls may not be man enough for the job!

🧍 **TWO BOXES OF TISSUES**

To have near the changing mat (babies pee at very inopportune moments when having a nappy change) and little boys go off like an unattended hosepipe!

🧍 **BABY WIPES/WATER WIPES**

Rather like a pack of pre-soaked tissues, these are handy to keep on the changing table. Travel packs are available for use in your nappy day bag. Try to find ones with minimal additives to avoid allergies/skin irritations.

🧍 **A SMALL BOTTLE OF ALMOND OIL OR COCONUT OIL**

🧍 **BARRIER LOTION SUCH AS:**
Neal's Yard Baby Balm
Waitrose Baby Bottom Butter

♦ TINY TROUBLES NATURAL INTENSIVE HEALING SALVE BY MAMA NATURE

Available on Amazon and the *best* nappy rash cure I have ever found! Whilst it is not cheap, you don't need to use much of it, and even then, only when they have a spotty botty.

♦ SUDOCREME

A rather more robust antiseptic cream for nappy rash — worth having around, but to treat existing nappy rash rather than as a preventative barrier.

♦ 4 OLD TOWELS

Hand towel size is fine or cut up old towels you never use. These are useful to have on a nappy changing mat to mop up little accidents like a random pee, poo or up-chuck whilst you are changing them.

♦ CHANGING MAT (EASILY WIPEABLE)

With removable towelling covers (get 4 covers): if you want, get 2, one for bathroom and one for changing table/ one for upstairs and one for downstairs.

♦ A CHANGING TABLE

Over-cot changing platforms are a pain to use if you can only position them with their feet against your front. It becomes more difficult to access baby's top end as they grow, and if they decide to poo and sneeze simultaneously during a nappy change, you will end up with poo all over you.

If you don't have a changing unit with drawers, then get some wicker/canvas storage baskets (not essential but can be useful to fill with all the above on the shelves under the changing unit). Don't underestimate the space you will need for both the growing baby and all the bowls/potions/cotton wool bags that you'll need to hand.

Top & tail basin or small plastic bowls

These are sold as a single unit in places like Mothercare, but any two small bowls will do. They're just for the water needed for nappy changes and face cleaning.

Laundry bags or bins

For the bathroom and nursery

Baby bath

Not absolutely necessary and a pain to store. If you have a normal size bath, there is no reason you cannot bathe the baby in there.

You might want the towelling covered baby "deckchair" support which sits on the floor of the bath. They can make things easier for a first-time mum.

Order from: http://www.amazon.co.uk/Baby-Best-Towelling-Bath-Support. The moulded plastic supports tend to make it very difficult to wash their backs or between their legs

♣ 4 BABY BATH TOWELS

♣ 2 SPONGES

Natural sponges are softer than the scratchy synthetic ones.

♣ A SOFT BABY HAIRBRUSH

Baby may be practically bald or have acres of hair, but either way it's nice to brush their head to improve circulation and can help if they get a bit of cradle cap

♣ BABY FLANNELS

They usually come in packs of 3 — handy for a quick face wipe or to cover a chilly tummy in the bath.

♣ BABY BATH THERMOMETER

♣ BABY SHAMPOO, A NICE ORGANIC ONE

♣ BABY NAIL FILES AND CLIPPERS

♣ JUMBO PORRIDGE OATS AND SOME POP-SOCKS

See section on Bathing for further explanation!

SWADDLES & CLOTHING

Babies grow surprisingly quickly during the first few weeks, so don't buy more than you need to start off with.

You may be fortunate enough to receive gifts or donations from friends, giving you a supply of newborn to three-month-old sizes for a while, so don't buy too much at the moment. Wait to see what you have at the end of the first week.

One thing that seems to be a common problem is that the sizes on many items of baby clothing (i.e. 0-3 months, 3-6 months etc) rarely seem to fit throughout that timeframe.

I mean, bloody hell! I'd be quite concerned if any of my babies was the same size at three months as they were at Zero; and as for a six-month-old still squeezing into a three-month old's sizing — forget it!

My advice is to simply buy Newborn size and then just upgrade to the next level when their toes start to look as though they are about to burst through the end of the foot bit, regardless of what it says on the label. In the case of vests, if it looks more like a Mankini because you are having to stretch it lengthways just to get the poppers to meet, it's time for a trip to the shops.

If your baby is on the petite size (premature or just a little less chunky than others) then Tiny Baby or Premature Baby size will do to start you off. (Unless your baby is petite, don't bother getting tiny baby size as they will be outgrown within about 2 weeks! Again, you may be given lots.)

6 x VESTS: NEWBORN SIZE

An all-in-one undergarment with little T-shirt or sleeveless style top half. Avoid buttons, they will drive you potty. Buy them with poppers at the crotch, "envelope" neck. Wrap-around style is nice if pulling vests over the baby's head is too intimidating for you at the start, but they'll have to get used to the over-the-head experience eventually, unless (apologies to any budding Billy Elliots out there) you intend dressing them like a ballerina for the rest of their lives.

6 VESTS: 3-6-MONTH SIZE

WINTER BABIES ONLY

A padded all in one ski-suit style onesie, with a hood.

BABY-GROWS

The all-in-one overgarment, patterned or plain, with all-in-one feet and long sleeves; ask for ones with built-in fold-over scratch mitts on the arms.

You will need about 6 of these to start with.

TWO NEWBORN SIZE DUMMIES, 0-3 MONTHS

I am not a fan of using dummies to silence babies when they are trying to tell you something important (or simply to send them to sleep), but they can be a Godsend when they are having a meltdown — just to calm them down.

GENERAL STUFF

BOTTLE STERLISING UNIT OR MILTON TABLETS
It is not necessary to sterilise bottles or breastfeeding equipment unless your water supply is contaminated. You can wash bottles and all feeding equipment in hot soapy water and air dry it; or put it through the dishwasher on a hot wash, storing everything in a Tupperware box until needed. Not essential to keep them in a box — just gives you easier access and keeps things tidy.

You can make up your own mind on this one.

Milton tablets in a bucket or bowl are helpful when away from home (overseas perhaps).

4 SMALL FEEDING BOTTLES (120ML/4OZ)
Find a make that your baby enjoys.

4 NEWBORN/SIZE 1 TEATS
Also buy some Size 2. You'll need them eventually.

4 X LARGE FEEDING BOTTLES (USUALLY 210ML/7OZ)

BOTTLE AND TEAT BRUSH
Bottle manufacturers usually offer a "starter pack" which includes both small and large bottles, as well as a bottle & teat brush. This tends to be a more economical way of getting all you need to start you off, so worth checking it out before buying it all separately.

Colourful baby gym/activity mat

You may be given one of these, so perhaps check out what people get you first — babies will enjoy playtime from 2-3 weeks old. Many people buy a beige or pastel one to go with their decor but given their limited eyesight, that is SOOOO boring for a baby — so bright colours, black and white for contrast and fun dangly toys are preferred. As hideous as they may seem to you, they will love it and so you might just have to suck it up for now. It'll be good tolerance-training for when they want to dress in lime green trousers and a shocking pink ballerina skirt to go to the corner shop!

Expressed breast milk storage bags

Breast pads - 2 boxes

2 Boxes of multi mam nipple compresses

A great soother for sore nipples during the early weeks of breastfeeding. Available in packs of 12 from Amazon.

Feeding Bras

Seek advice from a good retailer who will measure you correctly.

Sanitary towels/maternity Pads

Teena Lady do big and comfy pants which are ideal until bleeding settles down after the birth. Not exactly Agent

Provocateur, but my past mums swear by them; and frankly, if your partner has watched you giving birth then the pants will not exactly be a passion killer.

♦ PARACETAMOL TABLETS

♦ DISPOSABLE PANTS

♦ ARNICA TABLETS

Homeopathic remedy: great for pre-birth to post-birth bruise relief.

Start taking them a week or so before the birth, for around 10 days afterwards or following C-section. Breast-feeding mums have taken Arnica for years to help ease early discomfort.

♦ TEA TREE OIL

♦ MOSES BASKET WITH MATTRESS + 4 FITTED SHEETS

♦ CAR SEAT

Fully familiarise yourselves with how to get it in and out of the car. If it is Isofix it is pretty straightforward, but this is not something you want to start learning on the day you have to go to hospital. Master it and make sure it is in the car well ahead of the delivery date.

This is probably category Blue Job, mainly because it's bloody hard climbing around on the back seat of a car when eight months pregnant!

♁ STICK-ON CAR WINDOW SHADES

Don't put a "Baby On Board" sticker on your car. In my experience, most cars that display them drive like total twats, thus completely negating any warm and fuzzy feelings I might otherwise have had towards the drivers.

♁ PURE ORGANIC COCONUT OIL

A lovely moisturiser for you, your nipples and the baby's skin post-bath.

♁ TWO MEDIUM SIZED PACKETS OF FROZEN PEAS

(Yes, peas!) to be kept in the freezer. Engorgement can be pretty uncomfortable for a few days; regular application of a couple of bags of frozen peas, wrapped in a clean tea-towel will provide relief to the deeper tissue in the breasts.

FOR YOUR HOSPITAL STAY

♁ MATERNITY NOTES & BIRTH PLAN

♁ NIGHTIE/PJs/T-SHIRTS

♁ DRESSING GOWN

♁ 1 X BATH TOWEL

- 1 X **HAND TOWEL**

- 1 X **FLANNEL**

- **HAIRDRYER, HAIRBRUSH ETC.**

- **TOILETRIES**
  Toothbrush
  Toothpaste
  Moisturiser
  Facial wipes
  Toner spray
  Shower gel

- **WATER MISTING SPRAY**
  Hospital maternity wards can be really hot and stuffy.

- **MASSAGE OIL**
  Your partner might just give your feet/ankles a nice rub if you are hanging around waiting for Tiny Small to arrive.

- **FEEDING BRAS**

- **NIPPLE CREAM**
  The best thing is a pot of Virgin Coconut Oil (any good health food store).

Multi mam nipple compresses
You can take one of the two boxes mentioned earlier.

Silver breastfeeding cups
These are little cups which fit over the nipple and help protect them between breast feeds. They are made from pure silver which contains antifungal, antibacterial and antimicrobial properties. Silver also has anti-inflammatory properties and many of my clients swear by them.

Slippers/flip flops

Eye drops/lip balm

Socks

Disposable maternity pants

Mobile phone & charger

Sanitary towels & Bridget Jones-style pants
In case you are sore after the birth (or maternity pants).

Drink/food/snacks
You will both get hungry eventually!

Energy drinks/cordial/arnica 200 tablets, mineral water.

MAGAZINES

Remember, the Duchess of Cambridge had lots of help with that leaving-hospital look.

CAMERA

Make sure memory card is cleared!

CLOTHES TO COME HOME IN

For both you and the baby.

CAR SEAT

You are not allowed to bring baby home in anything else: practice using it before you actually HAVE to, even if you are taking a taxi home.

BABY'S HAT FOR TRAVELLING HOME

ONE SET OF VEST/BABY-GROW AND A BLANKET

For the home-coming journey. If a longer stay in hospital is needed, then bring more clothes for baby.

NEWBORN SIZE NAPPIES

99% WATER WIPES (ALSO KNOWN AS BABY WIPES)

BABY BLANKET

A cellular one is fine (the type with lots of intentional holes in) or perhaps a woolly or fleecy one in deep winter.

CHAPTER 3

TAKE TURNS AND PLAY NICELY

"PARTNERS CAN BE MADE TO FEEL THAT THEY MUST WHIP ON SOME
SUPERMAN PANTS THE MINUTE THEY COME HOME, INSTINCTIVELY
KNOWING EXACTLY WHAT IS EXPECTED OF THEM 24:7
'TIL, UM ... FOREVER".

Dear Reader ...

As instinctively helpful and supportive as many partners can be, we all know that some need a little nudge (or a shove) in the right direction from time to time.

I've witnessed many occasions when a partner breaks down in tears a few days after the baby arrives home, overcome with the responsibility that comes with being a new parent. This combined with the realisation of having to care for his partner on a whole new level can be terrifying.

A newly delivered mum can be a tearful and unpredictable being for a while, so it may feel like a turbulent time. Smiles and joy can quickly turn to tears and frustration. Reason and rational thinking go out of the window as everyone adjusts to life at home with a new tiny resident.

Unless one or both of them have been down the parenting road before, then we must assume that they are sailing uncharted waters. The following suggestions are some of the tips I have been able to give a floundering father in the early days. You are welcome to totally ignore them if you are indeed one of the Super Dads!

Try to imagine one of those wonderful little man-birds that you see on the David Attenborough documentaries. You know, the ones that dash about bringing their female counterpart twigs, bottle tops, feathers and bits of someone's discarded lunch. This is the man-bird being helpful and loving and probably hoping for a little bonus bonk if he makes a suitable impression on his muse! But under the circumstances, I think we can assume that bonuses of any kind are out of the question just now.

If you happen to be married to such an awesome man-bird type (Super Dad), then by now he may have already built you a table and covered it in morsels of fresh fruits dipped your favourite Green & Blacks organic chocolate, and therefore needs no instruction from me.

If not, then this task henceforth will be referred to as a Blue Job and duties must be shared if there is any hope of calm in the household.

As we live in a world where this book may be read by heterosexual couples, same-sex couples or single parents — I'm afraid, for the sake of simplicity, I will assume that the one who physically gave birth is the pink job person; the other is the blue job person.

If you are going it alone as a single parent, then you can delegate various jobs to your family members and friends as you wish; you will simply take on a kind of muddy, pale purple hue as you juggle between the two.

If the pink/blue delineation does not sit well with you, then perhaps think back to names of sports teams from your school days or famous couples and use those. Trojans & Spartans, Giraffes & Lions, Bonnie & Clyde, Butch Cassidy & The Sundance Kid — whatever makes you laugh and gets the jobs done!

Joking aside (but only briefly), partners often feel the same overwhelm as the mothers. They have quite possibly just witnessed someone they love, with every ounce of their being, going through a pretty tough few hours in order to give them *another* person they love with every ounce of their being.

If the birth was traumatic for the mum, it will certainly have impacted on their partner. It is important to discuss this, talking about how you both feel and make a promise to chat with the midwives/health visitor about it all in due course.

In the UK, talking therapy is available and can be a huge leap if you are somehow mentally stuck in the delivery scene, unable to move forward until questions are answered by those surrounding you during the birth.

If you feel that conversations about the delivery are making you anxious and tearful, it is a good idea to mention this to your health visitor so that a visit back to the hospital can be arranged. Here you will be able to speak to someone and they will be able to go over what happened and why, so that you can get closure.

Partners can be made to feel that they must whip on some Superman pants the minute they come home, instinctively knowing exactly what is expected of them 24:7 'til, um … forever.

So, let me suggest some blue jobs — a great way a new father can be supporting his partner while also adapting to his new role as Best Dad Ever.

Even in this day and age, birth and the period that follows it can feel a little coven-like, with the majority of midwives being ladies, mum friends stepping forward to offer advice, and grandmothers or female relatives doing likewise.

I have always made a huge effort to get the father involved in every way I can. Sometimes that entails almost dragging them upstairs to the changing unit where I can do a painting-by-numbers demonstration of a Top & Tail session or encourage them to deal with a rather intimidating Grade 8 nappy change. I also make sure that he is fully up to speed with what to expect over the first few days, arming him with a list of chores he can do to help support mum and baby, so making sure he is feeling both included and essential.

Seeing your tidy and ordered home gradually disintegrate, until it looks more like Day One of the January Sales at Primark is the reality for most people, but you can take preventative measures to minimise the fall out.

BLUE JOBS

Encourage her to drink plenty of water each day.

Put a thermos of cool water nearby and keep it topped up.

Do the same wherever she anchors herself, day and night.

Have a little Tupperware box or tin of snacks near her.

Make smoothies or juices; she may not feel like a large meal for lunch.

Make sure that your fridge is always well stocked with a variety of goodies.

Get a basic hit-list, you can set-up home delivery every few days.

Empty the nappy disposal unit every day.

Write down all the appointments needed to be scheduled (birth registration, midwife visits, family visits etc.).

Put laundry in the machine every time the basket starts to look full.

Change her bedding often, this will help her feel fresh and clean.

Take the baby from her during feeds and learn how to burp like a pro. While you do that, offer her a drink of water and something to eat. If your baby is fussing and proving tricky to latch, walk around with him.

- Keep a list of anyone who has sent a gift to the baby, as gifts start arriving.

- Change the water in vases of flowers every couple of days. Chuck out flowers that are wilted or smelling old.

- Run and empty the dishwasher as needed.

- Collect anything required from the chemist. Remember to take a list along of any other bits and bobs that are needed when you are out. If that mission falls between feeds, then perhaps pop the baby in the buggy and take him with you to allow your partner to have a shower in peace.

- Make sure she has a proper breakfast, lunch and supper every day. If you are not a good cook, ask someone to bring you meals for the freezer or source a delivery company who can bring you some healthy ready-made meals from time to time. While this is not cheap, it will buy you some much needed down-time now and then.

- Spend time learning how to collapse and re-open the buggy. Experiment getting it in and out of the boot of the car; do the same with any car seat that is not Isofix.

PINK JOBS

🤰 Feed the baby every 2-4 hours.

🤰 Burp the baby if your husband is not within reach. If your husband is within reach, then perhaps give him a pat on the back to burp him too!

🤰 Nappy change the baby if your husband is not available. He may be out or trapped in the car boot along with the buggy whilst trying to work out how it fits.

🤰 Worry for both of you, even though he seems quite calm.

🤰 Try to remember which side you last fed on. Then download a free breastfeeding app because you'll *never* remember which side you last fed on!

🤰 Write down all and any questions that pop into your head. You can have them to hand when the midwives come. Or, you can download a Voice Memo app because Sod's Law dictates that you'll rarely be in the same location as your notepad when these ideas pop into your head.

🤰 Rest, recover and heal. Remember, you've just built and delivered a baby.

You will both be shown a certain amount in hospital before you leave. The midwives will make sure you know how to change a nappy, clean the baby (both during nappy changes and daily top & tailing) and should give you support and guidance to ensure your baby latches well and correctly for feeding.

Sometimes you will have to ask for help, so don't feel shy to do so. Maternity wards are notoriously busy and demanding places to work.

Every new mother feels just as needy and lost as you might at the start, so push the buzzer and make sure you get someone to show you what's what.

CHAPTER 4

IT'S GOING TO STING A BIT

"TAKE THINGS EASY FOR A COUPLE OF WEEKS AT LEAST
AND YOUR BODY WILL HEAL MORE QUICKLY".

A straightforward vaginal delivery is what most women would wish for, but even with all the medical advancements made over the past few decades, complications are still quite common; your baby may still arrive into the world via the sun roof rather than the scenic route or following a long labour and the need for an episiotomy.

Your midwife will give you advice about how best to care for yourself in these circumstances.

Either way, you are likely to feel bruised and swollen around your undercarriage for a while, so you may find that this little tip helps give you some relief:

Pour a 2 x tablespoons of witch-hazel (available from a chemist) onto a thick sanitary towel, pop it in a plastic bag and into the freezer. Once chilled or well frozen, remove the towel from the bag and you can simply slide this into the gusset of your panties; this will provide you with some welcome soothing relief. Repeat as often as you feel you need it.

C-SECTION RECOVERY

Some mothers choose an elective C-section birth, perhaps wanting to have the certainty of the delivery date. Others simply have no desire to go through natural labour. Where a mother may plan for a natural delivery, circumstances can change during the labour, necessitating the need for a C-section.

Recovery times from a C-section vary hugely. I've had clients who are still pretty sore 4-5 weeks in, often as a result of infection or other complications, and others who are strolling down the towpath beside the Thames by the end of the second week. Try to acknowledge the fact that you have had major surgery on top of building a little human for nine months, adapting your recovery time accordingly.

When I started my career, C-sectioned mums were kept in hospital for a minimum of 5-7 days to rest and recover a little before returning home. These days, mums are usually sent home within 48 hours of the birth. As a result, the seriousness of the operation may be under appreciated. Because of the speed of such a turnaround, the perceived post-op recovery time is often diminished in the eyes of those around them. After all, how serious could it be if she is allowed home after a couple of days? The answer is: pretty serious.

A C-section is a surgical procedure, involving a horizontal cut through the fascia. This is a soft layer of connective tissue which acts as a sheath, covering layers of muscle.

Muscles will have been moved to the side, but not usually cut. However, they will have been hauled around in the birthing process.

After the birth, utilising those abdominal muscles to move from lying to sitting, or even just manoevering the baby during breast feeding can be extremely painful. The cut itself needs time to heal and although small, it can take up to six weeks for a mum to start feeling more mobile, so it is important to a) get as much help as you can during that time and b) don't rush things.

Enlist as much assistance at feeding times as you practically can. Having someone on standby to hand you the baby and take them from you for burping/winding etc. will be a huge help.

If your partner is home for a couple of weeks, then ask *them* to do the leg work up and down stairs to deal with nappy changes during the day. It is important to move about as soon as you feel able, but just take things gently.

The wound is bound to be painful for a while as it heals, but you should be sent home with painkillers to manage this for a week or two. Your midwife/health visitor/GP will be able to advise you of the best way to control any discomfort.

Do bear in mind that the use of any drugs may mean that you are tempted to do more than you should. Limit the number of trips you need to make up and down the stairs and if you are home alone.

For example, install a changing mat and all the clobber you

need downstairs for the daytime shift, along with extra nappies and changes of baby clothes.

Restrict trips out with the buggy to a gentle ten-minute stroll here and there for a while, gradually building up your strength and tolerance as you begin to feel better.

You may long to return to your previous fitness level, but by overdoing things you could well end up with internal problems and a wound that opens up a little. At worst, you'll have to return to hospital and I'm sure you don't want that. Take things easy for a couple of weeks at least and your body will heal more quickly.

We all know that sleep, good diet and rest aids recovery, so please take heed from someone who has seen many mums suffer as a result of being in too much of a hurry.

CHAPTER 5

HOLY SHIT — WE'RE TAKING IT HOME NOW?

"YOU MUST NOW LEARN WHAT HE NEEDS, HOW TO INTERPRET HIS CRIES, FEED HIM AND TEND TO HIS EVERY WHIM. IT'S A LOT TO TAKE IN".

In hospital, that dozy little bundle looked so peaceful and there was time to gaze lovingly down at your new child, while nurses and doctors bustled back and forth making sure everyone was OK. Cooing and fussing relatives and friends came and went, and all was well with the world. "I've got this", you thought.

The doctors, midwives, consultants and obstetricians, having been in and out of your life for the past nine months, must now fade into the background to prop up new mums-to-be.

It is time to go solo.

Guess what? They are actually going to let you leave the hospital. Yep, really! With your baby. Before you know doodly-squat about life on the outside.

No exam. No tests to see if you qualify as a Great Parent. No security tags. Zilch. Nada! Bugger all. They just let you stroll on out of that door. Just little old you. And a baby. That's all. You just walk … right … on …. out.

As you shuffle slowly to your car, you'll expect a gloved hand to grasp your shoulder whilst a seriously scary security guard growls, "And exactly where do you think you're going with THAT?"

It won't happen. Well, it might if that baby doesn't belong to you, in which case, Mrs Crazy Pants, you will have a shit load more to worry about than how to change its nappy!

So, let's assume the baby is yours and you are heading to your own car and then to your own home.

The first 24 hours at home with your new baby can be a time fraught with anticipation, angst and excitement. It's normally a huge relief to be back in your own familiar surroundings and only inches away from all your favourite foods/Prosecco in the fridge and, if you are anything like me, your own sofa to collapse onto.

Nonetheless, as the front door clicks shut and the clamour of the maternity ward fades to a distant memory, new parents often experience a wave of nerves as they start to anticipate the responsibility that lies ahead.

The sense that shit just got real, and that they have got to keep this new little human being alive settles firmly on their shoulders. They feel a little flutter in their stomach (which is clearly no longer a kicking baby!), so they take a big breath in and take their first steps into parenting.

Over the coming weeks and months, I can say with absolute certainty that you will become acutely aware of the parenting dichotomies out there.

People will politely, and usually not particularly subtly, grill you about your choices; frequently passing silent judgement with a twitch of an eyebrow, a slight downward and backward thrust of the chin or even a patronizing, head-tilted-to-one-side, "Oh, that's an interesting choice".

It starts with Breast or expressed?

Then EBM (expressed breast milk) or Formula (powdered milk)?

After you have finished feeling guilty or doubtful about that choice, they move to whether you are Demand Feeding, Attachment Parenting or "Aiming for a bit of a Routine".

Months later come the Michelin Starred Food Critics: Baby Led Weaning or Purées? Homemade casseroles or shop bought? Organic or whatever you can find?

Just when you think you are on the home straight, they will drill you about your "return to work" options.

Are you having a Nanny, Childminder, or sending them to a nursery?

It is an endless, waking nightmare of people unable to mind their own bloody business, but you will probably be far too polite to say as much.

For now, shut the front door and let it all soak in.

First things first — take a photo of your baby. It doesn't matter where ... in the car seat, on your lap or in your arms. You will never, *ever* come home for the *first* time with your *first* baby again, and in the kerfuffle that is the homecoming, you may forget.

Of course, in today's world of phone cameras, it is highly unlikely that your baby will so much as grow an eyelash without you taking a gazillion photos of the event — but the homecoming?

Awwwwww. Fuzzy feelings abound.

It's highly likely that you won't even remember that you have this photo until your child's 6th birthday, but it'll be nice to stumble across in a few years, if that turns out to be the case.

WHERE TO PUT THE BABY?

Most new mums feel a strong urge to have the baby in close proximity, certainly to start with.

It can seem a little gloomy to have gone through all the drama of the past nine months, not to mention the past few days, only to end up in an empty sitting room nursing a cup of really rather unpleasant Breastfeeding Booster Tea, while your baby snoozes two floors above you, oblivious to the potential for joy and celebration bubbling away on the ground floor.

Go on! Enjoy a bit of baby-gazing time and bring the Moses basket downstairs, until you feel ready to allow the baby some quiet time in his nursery.

Award yourselves a royal pat on the back and wallow in how clever you are, and how beautiful and perfect he is, then have a nice cuppa (or glass of bubbles) and breathe a sigh of relief.

If he looks a bit like a Pug-in-a-Rug, put the hood of the Moses basket up and take comfort in the fact that he will grow into that interesting little face soon, and you will love him regardless.

During the first few days following the birth, the baby is likely to produce some spectacular noises, most of which come from their nappy and will make you giggle (my family call them Brown

Sounds!), but some may make you rush to the crib expecting to find a gremlin instead of a baby.

Fluids which remain in their airways following the birth often take time to clear, so your perfect pink bundle might inhale and exhale a though he has smoked forty fags since yesterday. Coughs and sneezes, phlegmy deposits on your shoulder and sneezing are all necessary to oust any residual fluids and babies seem able to manage them very well without help from you. If they seem distressed or splutter a little when lying down, then pop them on your shoulder and have a stroll around the room until you both feel calmer again.

What do we do now?

You've done the first leg of the journey, and the next 6-8 weeks may be bumpy, so get ready for the ride of your life. Books describe the first few weeks as a "bit of a rollercoaster".

Even though this particular metaphor has been much over-used, it is accurate, and I can't think of a better one. You will have exhilarating highs, lurching twists and turns, whiplash changes of direction and occasionally end up at the bottom of a vertical drop feeling as though you want vomit all over your slippers.

You must now learn what he needs, how to interpret his cries, feed him and tend to his every whim. It's a lot to take in.

Selfishly, Mother Nature does not factor in a couple of weeks for you to spend languishing in a 5-star hotel in the Maldives, allowing you to have a breather before getting on with the next bit.

It would be nice to imagine that both Evolution and Mother Nature could sort out that particularly shite bit of postnatal planning in a few millennia. Perhaps we should get a petition going … if enough newly hatched women complain, who knows what we could bring about?

For now, just take another deep breath, unpack your bags and start getting to know your baby.

The Babymoon is over and sadly you are not going to the Maldives!

CHAPTER 6

WELCOME & UNWELCOME VISITORS

"ALTHOUGH YOU ARE ON A WAVE OF NEW BABY HORMONES AND WALKING ON AIR, YOU WILL BE TIRED".

Midwives and Health Visitors are a free service from our wonderful NHS. When you are preparing to leave the hospital, you will probably have been given an envelope containing your discharge notes, along with details of your Midwife Team. This should include a phone number which you can call at any time. If you haven't received this, then contact your delivery hospital and ask for it.

Will you get Miss Sugar & Spice or Ms. Vinegar Lips?

In recent years, I've seen midwives in London improve in the way they interact with my clients and I hope this applies across the UK. They seem to be getting better at engaging, allowing the parents to feel a little more nurtured and comforted.

On the whole, they are a good bunch and their job is to give you reassurance and support. Don't feel afraid to ask questions.

This is all new to you but old hat to them. A pimple on your baby's cheek (which definitely wasn't there this morning). A rash on their previously alabaster-like bum. That odd shivery thing they do when you are changing a nappy.

All these are quite normal and, almost certainly, nothing to worry about — but worry you will. So, ask away and by this time tomorrow you will have found something else to fret about.

It really ruffles me when I watch brusque, wooden faced, trained health professionals bark questions from their Q&A sheets, ticking off answers as though they are MI5 agents carrying out an interrogation, failing spectacularly to make eye contact with the sleep deprived and anxious couple in front of them.

Information leaflets about breastfeeding clinics, support networks and health checks get handed to you, with about as much interest as a fast-food restaurant server flinging you a menu, giving no explanation as to what they are about or why you may need them. Sometimes, they show scant interest in the baby other than to check for jaundice, weigh them or observe the latch for a couple of minutes before heading for the door.

I know that they are busy, and we *all* appreciate that the NHS is hugely overstretched, but I don't believe that this justifies the indifference still shown by some of the more old-school Midwives.

If you get a sour puss, just answer the questions and hope for a nicer one next time round. If you feel strongly about it, please do take the time to give feedback to your clinic. If no-one says anything, nothing changes.

Note to the Midwife or Health Visitor: If you are indeed a midwife reading this, then no matter how long you have been doing your job, or how many babies you have welcomed into the world, it will serve you well to be mindful that the trembling mum sitting in front of you knows very little; you know a good deal more than that.

Inside she may be nervous about your visit, worried that you are going to judge or criticise her. These mothers have real concerns that if they "give a wrong answer" or vocalise that they are finding it all a bit of a shit show, you might take the baby away from them. Mothers have told me this was one of their biggest fears in the early days.

Make eye contact, pay her a compliment (not just about the baby), ask her how *she* is and tell her she is doing great. If the baby has gained weight, even it is a small amount — rather than saying that the baby has "*only* gained 50g since your last visit", perhaps re-phrase and say "Well done Team — he's gained 50g since you were last seen. Let's see if you can beat that by my next visit on Wednesday!" Remember to include any partners in conversations and help them to identify their role in all this chaos. Again, I have seen health professionals direct all the questions at the ashen-faced mother whilst stonewalling the equally anxious new father sitting only a couple of feet away.

So please remember why you decided to become a midwife and be kind, be gentle, be present and inclusive.

National Health Service: In the UK, on arrival home, both baby and mother will be under the protective umbrella of this organization. This does not preclude you having your own private midwife, doctor or paediatrician.

Community Midwife: She will usually visit every two to four days, depending on how the baby is doing or can be contacted if there are problems in between times. She will make sure that the mother is monitored, that any wounds (e.g. episiotomy, C-section) are cleaned, are not getting infected and will regularly weigh the baby to ensure that feeding is going well. She will check the baby over, looking for problems such as nappy rash, thrush, sticky eye, sunken fontanel* or jaundice.

Health Visitor: Once the baby has regained any weight lost after the birth and the mother seems to be managing well, the midwife will sign her off and a Health Visitor will then arrange to call in. This is usually a one-off home-visit; however, the number of times a baby is assessed by their Health Visitor depends upon their general wellbeing, and how frequently the mum chooses to take them to a baby clinic for advice/to have them measured and weighed. Information will be given to the parents about immunisations, growth charts, details of the local baby clinics and any periodic health checks available. She will also speak about contraception (which is always good moment for a cynical cackle as you sit on your episiotomy cushion, having not been able to poo for two days).

*The fontanel is a soft indent in the top/mid-section of your baby's skull. This indent is simply where your baby's skull bones have not yet fused together. By running your fingers gently over your baby's head, you should be able to feel this little soft spot. A slight dip is normal. Please ask your midwife to explain more about the fontanel when she visits.

PERSONAL CHILD HEALTH RECORD OR "THE RED BOOK"

This is a record of your child's health and development over the first five years of their life. It is normally given to you either by your midwife or your Health Visitor. I recommend that you keep this permanently in the "Going Out and About" bag which is usually kept on or near your buggy. By making this a habit you will always have it handy if you need to rush to hospital/GP with the baby.

There are a minimum number of occasions when the Health Visitor and/or GP become involved between birth and age five, as part of the NHS child health surveillance programme.

The aim is to spot any problems as early as possible so that any necessary action may be taken.

The Health Visitor will inform the parents when these occasions are due. They usually take place at:

- Six to eight weeks
- Six to nine months
- 18 to 24 months
- Three to three-and-a-half years
- Four-and-a-half to five-and-a-half years

WHEN TO KICK PEOPLE OUT OF YOUR HOUSE

Although you are on a wave of New Baby Hormones and walking on air, you *will be tired*. The excitement of the new baby will carry you through the first few days, but if you overdo things during this time by having lots of friends visiting, you will quickly become exhausted.

Naturally, family and friends will want to come thundering over following the birth but try to bear in mind the enormity of what has just happened; not just to you as parents, but also to your baby.

He has to rest and recover and settle into new surroundings, getting used to the noises and smells of his own environment and begin bonding with mum and dad. There is plenty of time for fun and frolics after this settling in period and once the feeding is established.

It is better if parents can have a discussion about visitors, and perhaps discretely arrange a time limit so that neither parent nor baby get too tired. Perhaps a secret "code word" which can be used if either parent is feeling they are tiring or have simply had enough of a particular visitor.

New mums will make the mistake of overdoing things once or twice, feel shattered after a too-long-a-visit and not make the mistake again. It is a learning curve that most people go through and can be avoided with a little firmness and communication between family members.

DAD'S TIP

*When the time limit is approaching, one can tactfully step in with a smile and say "Can I make you one more cup of tea before you go? * I've got to make sure she has a nap." This way, visitors don't feel they are being kicked out, but the hint serves* *as a gentle reminder that mum, dad and baby need to rest.*

I stole this idea from my father. Lumbered with a gibbering female dinner guest who'd imbibed far more wine than was ladylike, he would escort her toward the front door, his right hand placed firmly between her shoulder blades as he deftly swept up her coat with his left on the way out, draping it around her. Then, smiling sweetly at her would croon, "Must** you stay? **Can't** you go?", at which she would simper and stagger off into the night saying "No, No. Really David, I **have** to go home! You are a naughty man", having totally missed the sarcasm. She was tipsy, happy and back again for more within a month!*

Many visitors are mums themselves, and they have simply forgotten how tiring it all is in the early weeks, so sometimes a gentle but kindly nudge towards the door is needed.

Remember, you are a new mother, not superwoman and even though you may have been a marathon runner or regular yoga guru prior to the birth, the body has to recover from both a natural or a C-section delivery, and this takes time.

Give yourself that time. Accept help when it is offered and don't try to return to your previous level of fitness in too much of a hurry. Being a good mother is not a competition, and no good will come of it if you do too much too soon! Don't compare yourself to other mums.

Mum: if you are breastfeeding, you are now the top of the food chain, or one of two main carers if bottle feeding. It is vitally important that you take care of yourself well, allow family or friends to help you wherever possible and rest as much as you can; make sure you fill your own body with a healthy balance of vitamins and minerals which will help sustain you.

You have many broken nights ahead of you; you will work harder and longer during the first 12 weeks of your baby's life than you have probably ever done on your own.

You **must** eat well, and you **must** rest whenever you can — even if just for a 30-minute nap. All those people who tell you to "sleep when the baby sleeps" really know what they are talking about.

I am fully aware that when you have had some well-rested friend telling you this for the umpteenth time, you will want to stab them in the eye with a bottle brush but listen to them! Don't argue about it, just go and lie on your bed for a while. If nothing else, it means you don't have to hear it for the umpteenth-and-oneth time. Once your baby starts crawling you will long for such an opportunity.

Buy a smoothie-maker or a good juicer perhaps, so that if you really cannot face a proper sit-down meal, you can take on a pint of cell-repairing, liquid energy a couple of times a day at least.

Get friends to make and bring over soups. A meal in a bowl. Perfect.

CHAPTER 7

SOME SERIOUS STUFF

"PLEASE, I IMPLORE YOU, TAKE THE TIME TO SEEK OUT A HIGHLY EXPERIENCED AND REPUTABLE PRACTITIONER".

JAUNDICE

Jaundice is a common and usually harmless condition in new-born babies that causes yellowing of the skin and the whites of the eyes. The medical term for jaundice in babies is neonatal jaundice.

Other symptoms of newborn jaundice could include:

 Soles of the feet and palms of the hands take on a yellow colour.

 The baby's urine appears dark yellow: a new born's urine should be clear.

👶 Poos are pale: they should normally be orangey-brown/ mustardy in colour.

The symptoms of newborn jaundice usually develop 2 to 3 days after the birth. It is generally nothing to be concerned about and the yellowing tends to disappear slowly over a couple of weeks.

WHEN TO GET MEDICAL ADVICE

Your baby will be examined for signs of jaundice within 72 hours of being born as a routine part of the newborn physical examination.

Should your baby develop signs of jaundice after this time-frame, contact your GP, health visitor or your midwife. Jaundice is usually nothing to worry about, but it is important to seek advice in case treatment is needed.

Keep an eye on the jaundice when you are home, and you should notice that day by day it lessens. However, if you notice the yellow colouring returning and your baby becomes disinterested in feeding, it is important to that you contact your midwife, GP or health visitor immediately.

WHY DOES MY BABY HAVE JAUNDICE?

The cause of Jaundice is a build-up of a yellow substance, called Bilirubin, in the blood. This yellow colouring is produced when red blood cells (carrying oxygen around our bodies) are broken down.

A newborn's liver does not function quite as effectively as ours do, so it doesn't do such a good job of removing this build-up of bilirubin; hence the baby's skin appears yellowed. Babies have a high amount of red blood cells in their little bodies, and these cells are broken down and replaced frequently.

Once your baby reaches about 2-3 weeks of age, their liver is much better at dealing with the bilirubin, and as a result the jaundice disappears with no harm done.

Occasionally, jaundice is a sign that there is some other health condition. This is often the case if jaundice comes on shortly after the birth; generally, within the 24 hours after the birth.

HOW COMMON IS NEWBORN JAUNDICE?

Jaundice is one of the most common conditions that can affect newborn babies, and I see it all the time in my day to day visits.

About six in ten babies have jaundice after the birth; and with premature birth (born before the 37th week of pregnancy) the number is around eight in every ten.

Only about one in every twenty babies will have a bilirubin count that necessitates treatment.

While there has not yet been any explanation for it, breast-feeding increases a baby's chances of developing jaundice; it can continue for a month or more.

The consensus of opinion in most cases is that the benefits of breastfeeding outweigh any risks from the jaundice.

TREATING NEWBORN JAUNDICE

The symptoms of newborn jaundice usually pass within 10 to 14 days, and treatment is not therefore required; but occasionally they continue a little longer.

If treatment is recommended, it is normally because test results have shown a high level of bilirubin in the baby's blood.

If left untreated, there is a **small** risk that the bilirubin could enter the brain and cause brain damage. But your baby will be regularly checked by your midwife team to ensure that he is within the safe zone, that the yellowing is receding over the time and if there is any need for treatment, you will be told.

By way of reassurance, over the past 24 years of working with my babies, I have only had two who have needed treatment, so it is quite rare.

Treatment types are:

Phototherapy: using a special kind of lamp, a light is shone onto the baby's skin, altering the bilirubin into a form which the liver can more easily break down.

An exchange transfusion: using a catheter (which is a thin tube) inserted into the baby's blood vessels, their blood is replaced with a matching donor's blood; if this procedure is necessary, the baby is normally able to return home after just a few days.

MASTITIS

You may have heard friends speaking about Mastitis, and whilst correct latch, good breastfeeding advice and breast care go a long way towards avoiding this, sometimes a mother can suffer this painful condition.

The breast tissue becomes inflamed, red, swollen and very painful. More often it only affects one breast, but on occasion both.

If you begin to experience flu-like symptoms such as:

- High temperature (fever) of 38C (100.4F) or above
- Shivering/Chills
- Aches

Speak to your midwife or GP. The onset of mastitis can be slow, so keep an eye on your breasts, regularly checking for blush marks and feel for small lumps which may indicate a blocked duct

There are two main types of mastitis:

NON-INFECTIOUS MASTITIS

This is usually caused by breast milk remaining within the breast tissue (milk stasis) as a result of a blocked milk duct or problems with breastfeeding.

INFECTIOUS MASTITIS

This is usually caused by bacteria. It is crucial that you seek help if you have any symptoms. If you don't then the condition could worsen, and non-infectious can become infectious mastitis; the possible cause being milk remaining in the breast tissue.

CONTINUE BREASTFEEDING WITH MASTITIS

Although it may not feel natural, and certainly not what you might want to do, it is important that you continue breastfeeding from the affected breast.

By continuing feeding you will:

👶 **AID THE REMOVAL OF ANY MILK FROM THE BLOCKED DUCT**

👶 **RELIEVE THE SYMPTOMS MORE RAPIDLY**

👶 **PREVENT CONDITION ESCALATING INTO SOME THING MORE SERIOUS**

Don't worry about the milk itself; it is perfectly safe for the baby to drink, although it may be a little more salty than usual. The baby's digestive system will absorb any bacteria present and will not cause any problems at all.

OUTLOOK WITH MASTITIS

In the vast majority of cases, mastitis can be dealt with using self-help. Make sure you rest, drink plenty of fluids, take paracetamol to deal with a temperature and alter your baby's feeding position. If you have been using a cross-cradle position to feed, then perhaps move your baby to the underarm hold. Ask your midwife to show you if you are not sure.

Ensure that your baby is correctly latched so that the breast gets properly drained. In some instances, your midwife may advise you to:

👶 FEED MORE OFTEN

👶 EXPRESS IMMEDIATELY AFTER A FEED

👶 EXPRESS MILK BETWEEN FEEDS

You can encourage the milk flow by expressing by hand or use a pump. You may find that a hospital grade pump (which can be hired from some chemists) may be more efficient than a shop bought hand-pump.

Infectious mastitis must be addressed quickly to avoid it escalating into something more serious, such as an abscess. In such cases, your doctor will probably put you on a course of antibiotics. If that is the case, then I'd recommend popping some infant probiotic drops into some cooled boiled water and, using a bottle, give this to your baby daily until you finish the course.

THRUSH

Caused by a yeast fungus called Candida albicans, thrush is an infection normally occurring in the mouth of a new baby. It is quite common in babies and children up to two years of age. It is uncommon for babies to have thrush during the first week, but it can develop around weeks two to three.

The first symptom you may notice is a white, furry looking coating on your baby's tongue which remains there long after the end of a feed. You may also find white spots across the roof of the baby's mouth, or on the inside of their little cheeks.

The white coating could simply be present immediately following a breast or formula feed, so if in doubt, check again in an hour or two to see if it is still there before hurtling off to the GP yet again.

Thrush spreads though the digestive system, so if it is left unnoticed in the mouth, it may appear in and around the baby's groin area; in this instance it is sometimes mistaken for nappy rash; however, nappy rash usually responds well to regular applications of products such as Sudocreme or Bepanthen, whereas thrush doesn't.

If the symptoms are still there after a few days despite using a nappy rash treatment, and you notice that their skin is slightly bumpy and peeling in that area, then Thrush could be the culprit. Head off to the doctor and, again, take advice.

Some babies can have recurring infections, in which case it may be that the baby is being re-infected by the mum, so it is worth seeking treatment for both of you (see below).

Oral thrush is not usually indicative of any other illness and often babies are not bothered by it. However, if it is present and seems sore, the baby may be tricky to feed if it causes them discomfort.

Speak to your GP and if treatment is deemed necessary, an antifungal medicine will be prescribed. This can be either a liquid, which is given orally through a dropper, or a cream which is applied by squeezing a little onto your index finger and smearing it around inside the baby's mouth. Some of these creams are quite yummy, with an orangey flavour — so in my experience babies positively gobble it up!

If you are prescribed antibiotics, as I advised earlier in reference to mastitis, it is a good idea to also take some pro-biotics to ensure that the baby's immune system is not affected. A breastfeeding mother taking antibiotics can have a knock-on effect. Your baby may produce runnier than normal poos and develop bad nappy rash.

Breastfeeding mothers may develop a thrush infection on their nipples and/or within their milk ducts. This can cause painful, cracked nipples and may make breastfeeding unbearable. If you think you may have a thrush infection on your nipples, **see a GP straight away**.

A first-time mother is unsure how breastfeeding *should* feel, so it is common for them to be completely unaware that they *have* thrush. It takes a little while to establish breastfeeding and, during that time, a certain amount of discomfort may be encountered.

When feeding, if you feel sensations such as severe
or sharp pain in the breast when the baby suckles,
this gives you a good indication that things are not
right. Arrange a visit to the GP as soon as you can.
It is possible that you have thrush in the breast.

If you are expressing and you are diagnosed with thrush, you should thoroughly sterilise all feeding equipment and pumps and regularly change breast pads. Change and wash maternity bras at least 3 x per day until the thrush clears up.

TONGUE-TIE & LIP-TIE

The frenulum is little ridge of tissue, connecting the tongue to the floor of the mouth or between the lip and the gum line. In the instance of a tongue-tie, sometimes it is shortened or even anchored right at the front of the tongue. This condition can be notoriously hard to spot and often not highlighted until they have feeding difficulties.

I've worked with many babies who, deemed to be tie-free by midwives, are later diagnosed with a posterior tongue tie which needed to be released. Often the mother and baby will have had to endure many miserable days before either giving up on breast feeding or finding someone reputable and experienced to do a thorough oral examination.

Babies who suffer with tongue-tie or lip tie will struggle to latch on. They will find feeding frustrating as they cannot suckle well and may fuss endlessly throughout feed times.

Cutting a tongue/lip-tie is a simple procedure which, once deemed necessary, should be carried out by the relevant medical experts. A laser procedure is far more accurate but perhaps not as readily available outside London.

If you suspect your baby has either of these issues, contact your health visitor to put you in touch with someone who will come to do a thorough oral assessment. They will advise whether the tie needs to be cut or whether it is better to leave it to resolve itself. In the meantime, using nipple shields may help make latching easier for the baby and less uncomfortable for you.

Unnecessary cutting can result in scarring which may make matters worse. Get it properly checked before going ahead; make sure you are given clear details about the aftercare needed to massage the scar tissue and manipulate the tongue following the cut.

Please, I implore you, take the time to seek out a highly experienced and reputable practitioner.

I once worked with a couple who simply used someone they found on the internet, against my explicit advice to the contrary. Apparently, the fact that she ran a breastfeeding café locally was enough of a qualification for them — and the fact that she was cheaper than visiting the specialist I recommended! The woman in question came to the house to do the procedure; the cut was made far too deep, the baby's mouth hemorrhaged, the mother was traumatised by the amount of blood and it resulted in the baby never being able to feed at the breast again.

STICKY EYE

A newborn's eyes often appear swollen and closed shortly after birth. This fluid retention drains away over the first 2-3 weeks and your baby will then start to open his eyes more to have a look at his new world. As babies have their eyes, nose and throat all contained in a small area compared to the adult human skull, drainage can be less than perfect.

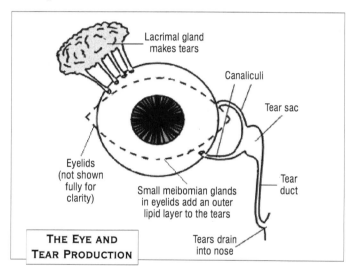

Lacrimal gland makes tears

Canaliculi

Tear sac

Eyelids (not shown fully for clarity)

Small meibomian glands in eyelids add an outer lipid layer to the tears

Tear duct

THE EYE AND TEAR PRODUCTION

Tears drain into nose

© EMIS 2011 - Author: Dr Laurence Knott

Normal tear production

The surface of the eye is very sensitive, so it needs to be kept moist and free from any dirt/dust if it is to remain undamaged. By producing a thin film of tears, comprising three layers — the middle watery layer, the thin outer oily layer, and the thin inner mucous layer — the eye remains protected.

The coating comes from glands which are situated just above and on the outer perimeter of the eye (lacrimal glands). This fluid drains out and across the upper part of the eyes, keeping them protected and lubricated.

By blinking, our eyelids spread our tears over the eye. Little glands located in the eyelids themselves (meibomian glands) produce a little oily liquid which in turn covers the tear layer. This keeps the surface smooth and helps reduce evaporation of tears.

Trickling on down the small channels on the inner side of the eye, they drain into a tear sac. From there, heading on down a channel known as the tear duct and into the baby's nose.

What causes a blocked tear duct in babies?

In a newborn, the most common cause is a bit of a delay in the opening of their tear duct. It is common and this occurs purely because babies are still a work in progress. i.e. they are not quite fully developed when they are born. Approximately 1 in 20 babies will have a tear duct that takes a while to develop.

How does it get better?

As with most newborn blips, time is usually the answer. As the baby develops, so the drainage will improve. However, if your baby is still experiencing pooled tears or gunky eyes after a few months, please consult your doctor.

Is it serious?

No, not normally. I generally find that babies I work with experience blocked or gunky eyes for about 2-6 weeks, after which it begins to clear up. Newborns don't produce tears to begin with (which is why you don't see them when they cry in the early days).

Unless the baby is unable to open their eyes, it does not seem to bother them unduly. You will probably find that it looks worse when baby has been asleep for a while, and the eye may be stuck shut in some cases.

As with most early-days issues, sticky eye will normally clear up in its own time. If the eyeball is clear, not bloodshot and the white of the eye is, well … white … then all is well. It can re-appear if your baby gets a cold (becoming blocked up again) but once free of any infection, normal drainage is resumed.

What should be done?

Gently massaging the outside of your baby's nose with your little finger, just in the corner where the duct is located, may help clear up any pooling. Make sure your hands are clean and repeat this process 2-3 times a day.

If any gunky or puss-like substance appears, you can gently wipe it clean with a little cotton wool dipped in warm water. You do not have to use cooled boiled water unless an infection is present, although you may prefer to do so.

If symptoms persist or you are concerned, speak to your GP.

Possible problems — conjunctivitis

You may find that the eyeball looks a little red from time to time. This inflammation is not normally anything to worry about.

If the condition worsens, it can develop into something called conjunctivitis. This tends to look worse than it actually is, and the eye can appear red from time to time, coupled with a constant stream of green goo appearing along the eyelid.

Conjunctivitis is not particularly serious, but it is infectious and will almost certainly need treating, so take your baby along to your GP. They will usually do a swab test and, if it is indeed conjunctivitis, they will prescribe an antibiotic eyedrop.

MILK SPOTS AND BABY ACNE

Milk Spots often appear on a baby's face after a few days. These little pimples are nothing to worry about; they are usually the result of maternal hormone fluctuations still in your baby's system.

These tiny spots appear like miniature whiteheads, often with a small red ring around them; usually just a smattering across the forehead, nose, chin and cheeks. These spots can be quite prolific, and usually get a little worse before they finally start to disappear.

Do not be tempted to squeeze or pick at them because this could result in infection and scarring. You will often find that they appear in the morning and are gone by lunchtime, only to reappear somewhere else the next day. As your baby's system settles down, so will the milk spots.

Baby Acne looks rather worse, often covering larger areas of the baby's face. It usually makes its first appearance when your baby is about 2-4 weeks of age. Baby Acne can last for several months and, much like Milk Spots, are a result of the mum's hormones still whizzing around the baby's system.

Remember, a baby's skin is highly sensitive, unlike that of us leathery, weather-worn adults, so it will take a while to develop; give it time.

The general advice for both of these skin issues is to leave well alone. Other than keeping his face cleaned daily with warm water and a nice pat dry, there is not much to be done. In severe cases, it may be necessary to contact your Health Visitor or GP who may prescribe some topical creams.

Some people suggest wiping a little breast milk, but the jury is still out on whether this is effective. Given breastmilk's seemingly endless benefits, not to mention wonderful microbial properties, it certainly cannot do any harm.

CRADLE CAP

Cradle Cap is quite common in young babies, but nevertheless it does look quite unpleasant. The scalp becomes dry, scaly and over time it may well resolve itself on its own. However, in some instances the skin can become quite thick, and cracked in appearance — rather like a fresh batch of chocolate brownies! In that case, it is worth trotting down to the doctor and asking if there are any specialist shampoos that he can recommend.

As a general maintenance programme, I suggest a gentle brushing of both forehead, scalp and even their little eyebrows (if they too are clogging up) using a soft baby hairbrush.

NAPPY RASH PREVENTION & CURES

Many years ago, before they put a man on the moon, we used towelling nappies secured with a safety pin. Convenience prevailed and now have all kinds of alternatives available from which to choose.

The ubiquitous disposable nappies are filled with tiny gel balls which absorb all moisture, wicking it away from baby's skin. This makes them the most popular choice, and certainly I rarely come across anything else in my day to day work.

Environmentally they are not ideal, taking years to break down in landfill, but that is a whole different debate. You can draw your own conclusions if you ever find time to play on the internet again! They are certainly convenient, quick and easy — all words we quite like when it comes to the early weeks with a newborn.

As your baby's little bottom will need cleaning several times a day, it is important to have good skin care products from the start. I have always made sure that for the first 2-3 months I apply a good layer of something pure/organic on a baby's bottom and around the groin area.

Do this with each nappy change. This ensures that you have a protective barrier in place between the poo and the skin, making it far easier and less abrasive than simply wiping poo directly off the skin.

Wipes and cotton wool etc. feel soft to the touch to us, but when used every few hours without a lubricant, a baby's delicate skin may become red and sore. Pee soaks into the nappy gel, so there is no moisture against your baby's skin. But poo simply dries up as the moisture gets absorbed into the nappy, leaving the residue stuck to the baby's bottom. This is why the lubricating layer is essential.

Nappy rash is something that may affect your baby at some point, but it does not mean that you are being neglectful in any way. It simply is part of life at this point. Make sure you have a few pots of creams to cover all options and you should be fine.

Barrier cream vs nappy rash cures

For many years I have used Neal's Yard Baby Balm, which is an almost clear lotion, not unlike Vaseline. I find this far easier to clean off each time than the creams that are heavier and white coloured (such as Zinc & Castor Oil).

Creams such as Sudocreme, Bepanthen and Metanium are creams intended to *treat* existing nappy rash as well as for preventative measures.

I have always sourced more natural and organic products to use on a baby's bottom, but from time to time you may have to bring in the big guns to deal with particularly stubborn nappy rash. This is down to personal choice. Nowadays there are hundreds of different manufacturers of wonderful baby products, so as fast as I write about them, more are flooding the market.

As with many other products, sometimes it is a question of finding what works on your baby. If shop-bought nappy rash creams do not seem to be calming the rash after a day or two, it is probably worth having a chat with your GP. It could be that the baby has developed thrush, in which case a suitable prescription cream will be given to you.

Sometimes skin conditions can take a while to be resolved. Try to be patient with your health practitioner while they find the right answer for your baby's skin type.

MENINGITIS

While Meningitis is most certainly not considered an "early day problem", I am highlighting it here because the onset is usually fast, serious and you should be made aware of it now.

One of the most concerning things about meningitis is that your baby could have some or all of the symptoms; they do not necessarily appear in any particular order. This makes it very hard to spot when you are a parent. An adult or child can verbalise that they feel ill, that their eyes hurt, or they have stiff neck, but a baby can't.

Symptoms of meningitis, septicaemia and meningococcal disease include:

🚼 A HIGH TEMPERATURE

🚼 COLD HANDS AND FEET

🚼 VOMITING

🚼 CONFUSION

🚼 BREATHING QUICKLY

- Muscle and joint pain

- Pale, mottled or blotchy skin

- Spots or a rash

- Headache

- A stiff neck

- A dislike of bright lights

- Being very sleepy or difficult to wake

- Fits (seizures)

A normal temperature in a baby is considered to be 36.4C or 97.5F but this can vary a little.

A fever is generally considered to be a temperature of 38C or 100.4F. If they have a fever, you will probably notice that they feel hotter than normal when you touch them, particularly on their back, tummy or forehead.

Babies may also:

- Refuse feeds

- Be irritable

👶 HAVE A HIGH-PITCHED CRY

👶 HAVE A STIFF BODY OR BE FLOPPY OR UNRESPONSIVE

👶 HAVE A BULGING SOFT SPOT ON THE TOP OF THEIR
HEAD

Someone with meningitis, septicaemia or meningococcal disease can get a lot worse very quickly.

The daughter of a close friend of mine was in the headlines in 2018 when her baby suddenly became ill at 3am. She noticed that her 9-week-old baby boy was not feeding; his body temperature rose quite dramatically, whilst his hands and feet remained cool. In the early stages there was no evidence of the rash, which is so often seen as a red flag for meningitis.

She contacted a local GP as soon as she could and was told that the first appointment was not until nearly midday. Luckily, she tapped into her new mum instinct which was telling her that her baby needed help sooner than that, so drove to her local hospital.

There she was seen by staff who failed to see the seriousness of the baby's condition and, as is sadly often the case with young, first-time mums, she was made to feel as though she was making a bit of a fuss about nothing. She waited and waited, not wanting to make waves.

Then, as she waited for a further hour and a half in triage to see a specialist, the rash appeared, spreading across his skin.

At this point the staff sat up and took notice at last; an ambulance was called, and she was immediately rushed to the Royal

Cornwall hospital at Trelisk, several miles away. Once there, her baby was immediately put into a medically induced coma.

He was given antibiotics as the Meningitis Team from the Bristol Royal Hospital for Children were scrambled and flown across the country to Truro. There they worked on the baby for three hours to stabilise him a little. He was then flown to Bristol for urgent, lifesaving treatment.

He had contracted the most severe form of the disease: meningococcal septicaemia.

The doctors at the Bristol Royal Hospital for Children said it was one of the worst cases they had seen.

Both mother and baby returned home several days later. At the time of writing, no-one knows if there will be any long term or as yet un-diagnosed damage to his brain. He is smiling, laughing and doing all the things a toddler of his age should be doing, but it is still too early to tell what the future may hold.

Please ensure that your Health Visitor gives you the leaflet explaining the symptoms and signs of meningitis. Copy them and pin them on the wall in your nursery or kitchen and make sure that anyone caring for your baby for more than an hour is aware of it. It moves swiftly and is very serious indeed.

When to act

👶 If you EVER feel your baby does not quite seem themselves, monitor them closely. No-one knows them better than you do.

If they are off their food, with a raised temperature, or floppy and lacking their usual sparkle, trust your instincts and take them straight to a doctor.

If you have to wait for a doctor's appointment, go to straight to hospital.

In hospital, make a BIG FAT FUSS so that you are seen quickly.

A normal temperature or fever is about 36.4C (97.5F) but his can vary a little. A fever is generally considered to be 38C or higher (100.4F). Act now!

If your baby has a high temperature take them to see a doctor as soon as possible.

If you have not already done so, for goodness sake, get yourself signed up to a Baby & Toddler First Aid Class as soon as you can. This is far more important than a term of Baby Massage and could save your baby's life one day.

CHAPTER 8

OSTEOPATHY & HOSEPIPES

"OSTEOPATHY (ALSO KNOWN AS CRANIAL OSTEOPATHY) IS A
HOLISTIC AND GENTLE APPROACH TO SOLVING MANY PROBLEMS
EXPERIENCED BY NEW BABIES, CHILDREN AND ADULTS".

My first and favourite osteopath explained what he was doing to me by telling me that my body was like a hosepipe! Now, I've been called lots of things in my life, but never a hosepipe. He went on to say that we "flow".

Our life force is a constant movement of energy around the body and for it to function at its best, it must not have obstructions. Where there are tensions or stresses, the flow just cannot work. Rather like running water through a hosepipe when someone is standing on it. It messes everything up.

"My job", he said, "is to take the foot off the hosepipe". A good, no-nonsense British explanation which I could get my head around at that time.

In Chinese medicine, it is called Chi, or Qi. That sounds a bit whimsy to us Brits, so the hosepipe analogy worked just fine for me. But Chi is life energy, a balance of Yin and Yang, and this flows through every living thing as bio-electromagnetic energy. Therefore, whether this appeals to your more in-tune-with-nature side or not, it sure as hell seems to work.

I cannot even begin to explain how, I just know that osteopathy has helped me and many babies in my care.

Osteopathy (also known as cranial osteopathy) is a holistic and gentle approach to solving many problems experienced by new babies, children and adults.

Since observing a treatment on a highly agitated and deeply uncomfortable little baby in my early days, way back in 1997, I have become a massive fan of osteopathy. I now visit my osteopath more frequently than I do my NHS doctor, although I must stress that there is a place for both when it comes to health and wellbeing.

From the patient's perspective, osteopathy amounts to little more than lying on a treatment couch while a therapist gently applies the lightest of pressure to relieve tensions in problem areas. This relaxing treatment encourages the release of many stresses which may be locked in the body. If the body is not operating as it should, it will find a way of manifesting that at some point.

For many years I have suggested that my clients take their new babies for a check-up with an osteopath, just to see if all is well after the delivery. Some babies found it difficult to alternate their head sleeping position, always facing right or left but never switching back and forth. Others were unable to feed because of the restrictions associated with tongue tie, suffered from reflux or trapped wind, a wonky hip alignment or overly curled toes.

Do bear in mind that while osteopaths can help alleviate many problems experienced by new babies, there are occasions when they can't. For example, if your baby is unsettled in the evenings or having a tricky morning from time to time, this is not something that needs "treating", because it is probably just your baby doing what babies do: challenge you from time to time! Osteopaths are great, but they cannot "fix" a baby when nothing is fundamentally wrong.

Mothers may also consider arranging a series of treatments for themselves both antenatally and postnatally to both help them prepare for and recover from the birth.

Sadly, it is not possible to clinically prove that osteopathy "works" in the same way that drugs companies strive to do by blinding you with scientific data and lab results. Osteopaths are therefore unable to promise that their treatments will solve any particular problem. I can certainly say that of all the babies I have taken along for treatment, most have seen either radical change or, at the very least some marked improvement.

The treatment consists of nothing more invasive than the therapist gently laying hands on the baby, using their highly trained fingertips to detect slight anomalies, tensions or restrictions in the membrane in which they are encased. With the tiniest of movements, they can release these blockages, easing tight areas so allowing the body to flow as it should. I've watched babies gaze at the therapists like a smitten teenager when they locate and initiate such a release.

My advice would always be to visit a qualified, recommended osteopath who specialises in the treatment of babies and newborns; do this as soon as you can after the birth. You have nothing to lose and, if it avoids months of misery and medicines, everything to gain.

CHAPTER 9

BOOBS & BOTTLES

"THE EASIEST WAY TO TELL THAT YOUR BABY IS FEEDING
WELL IS TO CHECK THE EVIDENCE IN THE NAPPY".

Right — I'm going straight to the point — no nipple pun intended!

Your baby. Your body. Your choice. No one else's bloody business. This can be your daily mantra.

I'm not going to get embroiled in the Breast or Formula argument here which is precisely why I used "&" rather than "vs" at the top of this page. It is not a competition or a battle. It is a personal choice and sometimes the introduction of a bottle is a question of necessity.

When coaching my clients, if they ask me what they should do, I have a standard reply: "Whatever works for you and your baby." Do your research about both to answer any questions you may have and follow your heart.

One does not have to be a nutritional expert to know that

breastfeeding your baby is the most natural way to go about things. I have worked with mothers who tried to give breastfeeding a go, yet found they hit all kinds of problems in the first week or two: mastitis, nipple thrush (which can be excruciatingly painful and usually puts a temporary stop to breastfeeding until cured) engorgement, cracked and bleeding nipples, lip and tongue-tied babies to name but a few. As a result, we have to move to bottles and formula to get us through until these problems are resolved.

Sometimes a solution is reached by getting mum up and running with the pump, so she can offer EBM (Expressed Breast Milk) from a bottle. This is a nice compromise for those who are still keen that their baby gets Mummy Milk rather than Formula.

Sadly, even the option of pumping may not bring the results needed. I've encountered many women who have tried expressing for up to an hour, producing no more than 10-15ml. In this instance, EBM is not going to be an option without spending many hours hooked up to the pump.

Also, you may not *want* to breastfeed your baby. (A sharp intake of judgemental breath from hundreds of breastfeeding advocates will be heard about now!)

There! I've said it.

You. May. Not. Want. To.

Breastfeeding is not the answer for everyone and not all mothers relish the idea of spending every 3rd or 4th hour rooted to the sofa day and night feeding their baby for months on end.

A handful of ladies I've worked with found the sensation of their baby sucking at their breast quite nauseating, moving to bottle feeding within a week; several felt that breastfeeding trapped them in the house, leaving them longing for company or just a bit of a social life now and then.

The fear of feeding a fractious and fussy baby in public can be unconquerable for some mums. So much so that even the most efficient feeders may bolt for the privacy of their own home, rather than sit in a crowded café or restaurant.

It is a sad fact that even in our more enlightened times, there are still some really ignorant people who will suck their teeth or glower at a breastfeeding mum in a restaurant as though she is dismembering a hamster on the table; she's simply holding her baby close while he feeds.

This attitude does little to help new mothers creep out of the house and start mixing with the daylight people. Teeth-suckers and glowering morons must seriously *get over it* ... or be firmly told to look in another direction if it bothers them that much!

Given that newborns usually need feeding every 2-4 hours to begin with, the logistics involved can leave a new mother feeling she can barely leave her home. If this happens to you, you might think about seeking a mum-friend who is ahead of you in the game. She may well be up for coming out on some café recces to build your confidence.

Studies are being published at a rate of knots about the pros and cons of breast vs formula, so as fast as I write, there will be yet more conflicting advice for you all to chew on. It'll give you something to read during the night feeds!

Some of my mums really enjoyed their breastfeeding time, but others said it they found it mind-numbingly dull. Plenty more managed to land on a middle ground, being able to happily mix breast and formula feeds over 24 hours. This meant that partners, doting friends or Grannies could get involved with the feeding on occasion, giving mum a bit of respite, time to sleep or grab a shower; everyone was kept happy.

Whatever way you choose to feed your babies, remember it is: Your baby. Your body. Your mental health. Your bloody business.

> "Don't let the noise of others' opinions
> drown out your inner voice."
> *Acknowledgement to Steve Jobs*
> *for this little peach of a quote.*

I've covered breastfeeding in this book, and I will also include bottle/formula options. When it comes to keeping everyone happy, the subject of how to feed our babies is as volatile as Brexit and Climate Change rolled into one. A country divided, and everyone thinks they are right. Pick whichever method you want and scribble through the rest with a pen.

As there are generally more physical challenges for breast feeders than there are for bottle feeders, I am going to cover breast feeding first.

THE PHYSIOLOGICAL BIT

Breast milk is made in response to the baby suckling at the breast and by the hormonal changes after delivery.

Milk is made and stored in clusters of cells in the alveoli of the breast (see diagram).

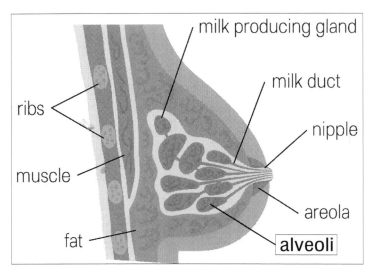

Each time the baby suckles at the breast, a hormone called **prolactin** is produced. High prolactin levels encourage milk production and a good supply of milk.

Another hormone, **oxytocin**, is produced shortly after the baby starts to feed. This creates the "let-down" of milk from the alveoli, down the lactiferous ducts and is then readily available for the baby as he sucks. The let-down reflex determines how quickly the milk flows, and therefore, how long your baby takes to feed.

. As the breasts empty, prolactin enables the breast to immediately start to make more milk for the baby's next feed.

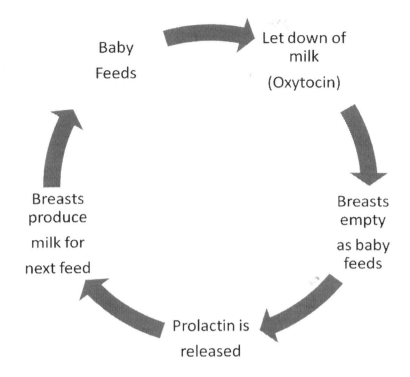

Baby Feeds → Let down of milk (Oxytocin) → Breasts empty as baby feeds → Prolactin is released → Breasts produce milk for next feed → Baby Feeds

GETTING STARTED WITH BREASTFEEDING

For many first-timers, breast feeding is second nature and both mum and baby just click. Engorgement comes and goes within a few days and the baby latches and feeds well without any trouble.

Being infinitely portable, breasts mean that you don't have the hassle of having to clean and make up bottles several times a day and if you can express, gives you the added bonus of being able to leave your baby with a family member or friend for a few hours now and then.

Realistically, hundreds of mothers find breast feeding far from easy. In fact, they find it bloody hard.

It may be the most natural way to feed a baby, and if it works for you and your baby, then Hurrah! But for the others it is often an emotionally draining, extremely painful and sometimes humiliating experience. This is not made easier by the huge amount of pressure currently applied to new mothers to exclusively breast feed.

I have witnessed mums who have felt so brow beaten by breastfeeding advocates that they have then pushed themselves beyond their physical and mental limits; ending up with any shred of confidence they had in tatters, they find themselves teetering on the brink of PND, if not pushed over that brink completely. This cannot be right.

Most natural, yes. Best? Hmmmm. I'd factor in how it impacts on the overall mental health of the mother in the bigger picture.

The bottom line is if you have a baby who is crying for food, they must be fed. If you are having trouble with breastfeeding in the early days and really want to persevere, then I urge you to find an open-minded expert to help you. Make sure you quiz them thoroughly to make sure they will support you, whatever method you choose, before inviting them into your home.

There is no shame in seeking support and it may make a world of difference to your experience. In the interim, please don't feel bad about offering your baby formula feeds whilst you get the breastfeeding problems under control. A fully fed baby is usually a more content and calmer one, and that alone will help you feel a whole lot better about everything else.

Some of you will have attended an antenatal class; most first-time mothers do. You may have spent some time giggling at demos done with a couple of dummy silicone breasts (or knitted ones if your class was a bit old-school), so this may be familiar territory. It's all well and good being shown with either a dolly (or aforementioned squishy boob) how to establish the perfect latch, but neither of those examples can replicate a squirming, shouty little lap full of ravenous impatience will they?

I have long since realised that *explaining* how to breastfeed vs. actually breastfeeding are worlds apart.

When in hospital, you may have to nag a bit to ensure that someone spends plenty of time helping you in the first day or two. Without the right guidance you can end up with a poor latch resulting in very sore nipples. If you don't feel confident (and many mums don't to start with), then ask again until you are.

If you are sent home before your milk has come in, it's well worth the money to get a non-judgmental, breastfeeding expert* in to show you how to position your baby as early on as possible. They will identify any problems, guide you with positioning and help troubleshoot a difficult feeder in a much more relaxed environment than a busy postnatal ward.

Good contacts are:
- Your Midwife Team
- Your Health Visitor
- The National Breastfeeding Helpline: 0300 100 0210
- Geraldine Miskin: www.geraldinemiskin.com*

When does the milk come in?

Normally between Day 3 & Day 5.

From mid-pregnancy onwards, the breast produces *colostrum*. This is the pre-milk which the baby will drink for the first few days after the birth. With a very small tummy at this point, he will want to feed little and often.

This is why Mother Nature does her usual magic and makes sure that the first few feeds are luxuriously rich. The naughtily unctuous end of the breastmilk spectrum — rich, concentrated and high in calories, the baby will only need small increments now and then while he recovers from the birth and waits for the milk to come in.

On average, it takes between 3-5 days for a mother to start feeling her milk coming in, so be reassured that the colostrum and feeding every 1-3 hours will usually satisfy your baby until that point.

If you have a particularly hungry baby, please don't feel you are failing in some way if you offer him a bottle of formula to tide him over until your breasts get up to speed. It is readily available if a baby is hungry, although one of my clients pointed out that some hospitals will not offer it unbidden — you have to ask for it!

If you have read the earlier section of this book about getting prepared for the Homecoming, by this point you should have some packets of peas to hand in the freezer. Now it will start to make sense.

As the milk starts to come in, the breasts often dramatically increase in size. One father insensitively referred to this happy day as "The Arrival of the Titty Fairy". A comment that was not well received at the time and resulted in a wooden bedside lamp stand being hurled across the room! Dads/Partners perhaps it's advisable to just button your lip!

At this point you may experience some discomfort. As the breasts fill, they may become hot and tender and very sensitive.

Until now the baby has been happily gorging on colostrum (and perhaps formula top-ups), but now he's going to upgrade to Mummy Milk; by offering evenly spaced feeds every 2-3 hours, your baby and your breasts will start to find a Supply & Demand rhythm which will gradually see a reduction in frequency in this initial phase.

Some tips to help with any discomfort:

- Before each feed, pop a hot flannel (face cloth) over the nipple area to soften and relax the tissues.
- After each feed offer cold compression using the packets of frozen peas (or something equally cold) wrapped in a tea-towel on/around any hot and uncomfortable areas of each breast for approximately 10 minutes. There are breastfeeding shaped gel packs available, but I find that they just don't stay cold for long enough to penetrate deep into the breast tissue.
- Savoy or white cabbage leaves applied to the engorged breast — they can be slipped inside the feeding bra to cool and reduce inflammation.
- Encourage the baby to feed well and often — every 2-3 hours in the early days. This will lengthen into 3-4 hourly as the milk flow settles down.

- Drink plenty of water as this will encourage good milk flow.

This discomfort usually only lasts a few days at most; less than that if you get a nice well-spaced rhythm going rather than frequent snacking bouts.

If you are still struggling after a few days or your nipples are becoming cracked or beginning to bleed, then you must seek expert help. In the meantime, you could try using nipple shields to make feeding less painful. You will need advice to ensure you buy the right fit for your nipples, so speak to your midwife or breastfeeding advisor.

It is essential at this stage to keep the baby feeding regularly and well from each breast. To start with, try offering the first breast for 15-20 minutes, then having a little break during which you can see if he needs a little winding.

I often find that babies are quite dopey halfway through a feed, so a pause to do a quick nappy change will not only rouse them for the second side, but often helps move stubborn bubbles around to help bring up reluctant burps.

If you notice tiny specks (like coffee grounds) of blood in any regurgitated milk from your baby, it is usually simply a result of the engorgement causing tiny ruptures of your own capillaries deep in the breast tissue. The dried blood mixes with the milk as the baby feeds and, as your breasts settle down this will stop. It is nothing to worry about.

Put your baby to the breast whenever he wakes for a feed/appears hungry. At the moment it will feel difficult for you to identify whether he is hungry, windy, tired, poopy or just plain grumpy. You will gradually get the hang of each other, so try to relax.

Of course, the best possible start is achieved by getting an expert in to work with you. They will show you how to establish correct positioning and check for any oral impediments which may hinder a good latch.

Ideally, try to seek out someone who is open minded about breast vs. formula; some mothers simply cannot produce enough to satisfy their baby's appetite. The last thing you need at this fragile stage is a strident pro-breastfeeding expert who will not entertain the prospect of mixed feeding and views formula milk as the food of the devil.

While it is hardly a great revelation that breast milk is the most natural thing to feed your baby, it is not the *only* thing you can feed your baby. Moreover, formula is not snake poison, simply Silver Top milk rather than Gold Top; when it comes to food choices six months down the line, unless you are planning on presenting your little darling with organic, home grown and home cooked food for every single meal, then it's a good time to embrace being a little open minded.

The most important thing is to get food into the baby for now, and the rest will follow.

When you are sitting comfortably:

👶 Offer the breast and do your level best to ensure a good latch, and that he only gets to **stay** attached if he has achieved the correct latch.

- If he hasn't but has taken an age to get on at all, don't be tempted to say, "Oh, that'll do". He won't feed with maximum efficiency and you will end up with sore and possibly bleeding nipples within a day or two.

- If it doesn't look right or is painful for more than just a few seconds, then chances are he hasn't got a good latch or may have a tongue-tie/lip tie. Using your finger in the corner of his mouth, break the suction and take him off.

- Try again until he goes on correctly. He is learning, but as Mum, you are teaching and learning simultaneously. Be patient with yourself and with him.

- If necessary, wait for him to start to get a bit shouty (capitalizing on the opportunity presented by a wide-open mouth), then snap him on! He may grump for a moment or two, but with a bit of luck and a little perseverance you will see him start to suck.

- Watch his temples; they should sink a little with each pull. Also listen for the swallow. Where mums have a fast flow, babies do a swift suck-swallow 1:1, if your flow is a little slower, your baby may take 2-3 pulls, scooping up a bigger mouthful of milk before swallowing.

Feed baby on one side, for 15-20 minutes, ensuring you pause now and then to see if you can help him bring up some wind.

It is a myth that breastfed babies don't need to be burped. Some of my past babies have belted out proper builder's burps as they fell off the boob. Also, it is worth knowing that regardless of whether they are breast or bottle fed, some babies need more frequent burping than others. If there is simply no burp to bring up, then no amount of back-patting will create one.

Make sure that you are keeping an eye on him while you get to know how he feeds. Try to avoid distractions while you are both learning so that you can monitor how well he is feeding. If you are mucking about on your mobile phone with one hand, you are not concentrating on how much he is taking. While you are busy catching up on your Text Message chat, he might be a-snoozing on there. Just saying!

After the first 15-20 minutes is up, you might find that he is quite dopey. Take him off the breast and do a nappy change to awaken him, then offer him the 2nd breast for a further 15-20 minutes. After all that, your feeding hour will have flown by and your new baby will probably be ready to go back to sleep.

Breastfeeding is a highly individual experience, so you may find that your baby does 20 mins on one side and 10 on the other, 20 mins on each side or even a whole feed on one breast, moving over to the other side at the next feed. Mix it up and see what works for you and your baby. There is no one-size-fits-all here.

Remember, your baby is still tiny. Playtime is not going to appear on his radar for another 2-3 weeks at least, so don't be concerned if he feeds and goes back down to sleep quickly afterwards. It is during these lovely sleeps that babies do the majority of their growing, resting and digesting; it's just what they need. Enjoy the free time while you can!

You may find it helpful to download a free breastfeeding App which you can use to keep an eye on the timings, frequency of wet/dirty nappies and general patterns.

Days do become pretty repetitive and as you get more tired, it becomes harder to keep tabs on which side you started or ended with and for how long the baby fed. If you are not tech minded, then keep a little notepad near you during feeds to keep track of things.

Contrary to what you may believe, babies frequently fail to leap onto the breast like experts — indeed many of my clients have several days of frustration and tears whilst getting the hang of it.

Sometimes I roll my eyes in wonderment as I watch a baby frantically trying to locate a nipple just millimeters from their top lip, whilst turning their open mouth towards the mother's guiding thumb resting on their cheek. As a species, its nothing short of a miracle that we humans have made it this far up the evolutionary ladder. I despair of them sometimes, yet they make me chuckle with their frantic impatience at the start.

Keep reminding yourself that you are new to this; it can leave you feeling a bit panicky when he is shouting for his meal and you are not feeling super-confident in getting it organized for him. Cut yourself a bit of slack, take a deep breath and stick with it.

Newborn babies cannot see clearly. They rely almost entirely on touch, sound and smell to work out their world. Hence the suck reflex is nature's way of making sure that if they can't see a nipple, they can locate it by touch. You just need to give them a little help to start off with.

Feeding 2-4 hourly at first, you may move to 3-4 hourly feeds after a week or two. Regularly spaced and frequent feeds will send the message needed to your breasts to produce milk.

Don't put a strict curfew on the end time but be mindful that if he is still hanging off your nipple after 1.5 hours, yet not visibly suck/swallowing, then you are being used purely for comfort.

It is important to remember that you will be encouraging poor sleep associations if they continually fall asleep at the breast while not feeding. If this is how they learn to fall asleep now, you may find it harder to settle them without feeding them to sleep further down the line.

This new supply of milk is what will sustain the baby from

now on. As the baby comes to the breast, sucking quickly to start with, he will get a few minutes of foremilk — the watery First Course, if you like. Once the hind milk is reached — the richer and thicker Main Course - his sucking will slow down a little to a more rhythmic pull on the breast, with his jaw moving up and down and a pulsing depression visible in his temples. This means he is feeding well.

Milk production works on the principle of supply and demand. The more need (stimulation/feeding) there is, the more milk the breast will make.

Note: Breast size has no impact on how much milk you can produce. However, it does affect how much milk you can store. This is why some babies can take a full feed from one side, but others need to be offered one side then the other.

Having flattened nipples (which can be hard for baby to pull into their mouth cavity) or inverted nipples (which turn inwards) does not necessarily mean that a mum is unable to breastfeed, but she may need extra help in getting started. Babies breastfeed by encompassing the areola, *not just the nipple.*

If you focus on getting the right help in the early days, ensuring your baby latches correctly and feeds for the correct amount of time to fill that little tummy, then you should minimise problems. Doulas, Health Visitors, private breastfeeding experts and the NCT are all good places to start.

Inevitably, one has to accept that there are times when the amount of milk you are producing is not enough for your baby to gain weight. When you are tired or before your milk comes in, for example. In that situation, there is no harm in offering your baby some top-ups of formula from a bottle to get you over a rough patch. Once you are more rested and relaxed, you may be surprised how things might improve.

There are several ways that you can boost your milk supply: expressing your milk can increase supply, but it is typically recommended that you don't start regularly expressing until your milk supply/demand pattern has settled down. This can take about 2-3 weeks. Alternatives are milk boosting teas or capsules such as Fenugreek._

Most mums will worry whether their baby is getting enough at each feed. When offering a bottle feed, you have the reassurance of being able to see the amount at the start and end of each feed, seeing the milk draining away before your eyes.

Winding or burping

You may have heard that a breastfed baby doesn't need to be winded. Sorry, but I disagree and, having worked with over 6,000 babies, I think that experience counts for something.

I have found that most babies need a bit of help to bring up trapped wind during and after feeds, certainly in the early weeks. Some burp readily and some need a little support and encouragement to do so.

Their digestive tract is still a work in progress and the sphincter pylori, which is found in the stomach, is the muscle responsible for preventing food from travelling down into the small intestine until the baby's tum has done its job, which is to mix the milk and the digestive juices together.

This sphincter muscle eventually becomes strong enough to prevent those yoghurty possets ending up all over your shoulder, by keeping the stomach contents where they should be.

Some babies feed incredibly fast, gulping at the breast or bottle as if they only had minutes to eat, and likely to result in their swallowing a certain amount of air at each feed.

If the baby is allowed to continue feeding at this pace, then it is only a matter of time until the resulting bubble begins to cause them discomfort. They will pull away, possibly crying and wriggling with the pain. I'm sure most people have experienced trapped wind at some point in their lives. It is pretty uncomfortable for us as adults, so for a baby, it is rather like having a nasty stitch.

The best course of action is to remove your baby from the breast or take away the bottle every few minutes, sitting your baby upright on your lap, or over your shoulder for a few moments to allow them time to have a breather.

There are various techniques you can try, so perhaps have a look on YouTube for some inspiration, or simply experiment. There is no right or wrong way, and your technique may differ from your husband's/partner's.

Don't hold your baby upside down and use common sense. If he is folded in half, then any bubble trying to head north will simply stay put. The bottom line is that as long as you get a nice big burp, job done.

If baby seems calm and dopey, not giving any indication of

discomfort, then there is no point trying to get a burp up. There may not be one there at all. But it is always a good idea to break the feeds here and there to give them a chance to release even the littlest of puffs.

EXPRESSING MILK USING A PUMP

It is generally advisable to wait for a period of about 2 to 4 weeks before you tackle pumping. By then a rhythmical supply and demand feeding pattern may have been established with breastfeeding.

Assuming that you are not trying to overcome issues such as mastitis or sore nipples you might want to have a go at expressing some milk earlier than this.

In London, it is possible to hire a hospital grade pump, and this may prove more efficient than some of the shop-bought models. Cost-wise it is worth doing a comparison, calculating the weekly charge for hiring versus the total cost for buying a double pump. Check with your Health Visitor to see if the rental option is available in your area.

Using a pump looks pretty straightforward. However, psychologically speaking, attaching yourself to a battery-operated machine can leave you feeling a little like a dairy cow.

It is certainly not glamorous, but it could be a lifesaver when you are faced with the demands of unsettled evenings or during growth spurts.

Growth spurts are periods when your baby suddenly needs to

feed more frequently, thereby increasing the amount of milk available to him (when breast feeding) and so meeting the demands of his rapidly growing body. If you are feeding your baby with formula, you will probably notice that he is regularly draining the bottle and still looking round for more. You simply increase the amounts you are giving him at this stage. I will go into growth spurts in more detail later in the book.

The increasing frequency of feeds at that time can be exhausting, so having enough expressed milk banked in the freezer could mean you can meet this increased demand, by offering the baby top-ups rather than feeding more frequently. It also allows your partner to enjoy feeding your little one and gives you a green light to have a blissfully long bath, a good block of sleep or just catch up with emails.

With a double pump and a specially designed pumping bra, you can drain both breasts simultaneously. I'll be honest here — a double pump bra set-up is more Lady Gaga than Victoria Beckham in the fashion stakes, but it does mean that you can crack on with work on the computer or blow dry your hair at the same time.

Once you have finished, you simply pour the resulting amounts into breastfeeding bags, label them with dates and quantities and put them in the freezer to use as needed. Oddly, they also have

Name: ....

... as one of the things you fill in on the bag. One dad I worked with suggested that it was for chaps who name their partner's breasts, like Pinky & Perky or Wallace & Gromit. Probably the same dad that got the wooden lamp shade thrown at him!

Even though pumping looks quite straightforward, some

mothers struggle to produce very much despite their best attempts. If this is the case for you, then perhaps you need to rethink things.

If you're feeding your baby for an hour, having to wait an hour before your pump yet trying to aim for feeding 3-hourly, this really doesn't give you much time to do anything else. If you pump and your milk flows quickly and easily, then this is great, but I would not recommend that you run yourself ragged to produce a small amount.

If the whole point of the exercise is to give you some respite, then this clearly is not going to do the trick, is it?

As I said above, having a readily available store of frozen milk will come in handy when the baby hits one of his many growth spurts. Until the breast can respond to the increase in demand (i.e. more frequent feeding), it's convenient to have a bit of back up in the freezer.

If you have been unable to produce milk by pumping, then the options are to offer feeds more often or formula top ups until the breasts catch up.

Taking care of your breasts

Having a hungrily feeding new-born attached to your breasts over the first few days can take its toll. Nipples can become sore and, if the latch is not correct, can result in the nipples becoming dry and cracked. This is very painful and, with the proper management, can be prevented.

In addition to the hot & cold compressing mentioned earlier, it is advisable to have the following to hand, just in case:

NIPPLE SHIELDS

These help when the baby finds a latch difficult or when your nipples are sore and in need of a break.

PRO-BIOTIC POWDER + BREAST SHELL

You can use this in case you get thrush on the nipple (make it into a paste apply to the nipples after each feed).

HYDROGEL PADS

Pads are soothing for nipples.

MULTI-MAM NIPPLE COMPRESSES

They come in packs of 12 and are available from Amazon.

COCONUT OIL

A great resource to moisturise nipples.

CHAPTER 10

IT'S MILK POWDER, NOT POISON!

"IF YOU ARE PURELY BOTTLE FEEDING, THEN IT IS JUST A MATTER OF TRIAL AND ERROR UNTIL YOU FIND THE SHAPE YOUR BABY PREFERS".

There are plenty of formula brands on the market; it is not my place to tell you which one will be best for you. Perhaps buy one of the more popular brands and see how you get on.

If your baby has any allergies or intolerances, your GP/Paediatrician will guide you towards suitable makes for your baby.

In all my time working with newborns, I have not yet come across a baby who has a problem mixing breast and bottle, so I'm afraid I don't subscribe to the "Nipple Confusion" argument. Preference perhaps, but confusion? No.

As long as you introduce a bottle to a baby early on, then it is usually quite simple. It is worth noting that you must maintain the bottle feeds as a regular feature in their week if your baby is to remember how to switch between the two.

If you suddenly drop it from the curriculum for 2-3 weeks, you may find that your baby *forgets* how to feed on a bottle, and it'll take a little persistence to re-familiarise himself with it. The same can also happen in reverse. If you were to go away for a weekend and leave the baby with a doting grandmother and a freezer full of EBM, you might find that on your return your baby shuns the breast having found a much quicker route to a full tum. Swings and Roundabouts, girls.

If you offer a feed every time he is unsettled or grumpy, then you will likely be giving him more to eat than he actually needs, and this could lead to him gaining more weight than he should.

Instead of making food the answer to every whimper or whine, spend time getting to know your baby and you may see that simply helping him off to sleep, or removing him from a stressful or noisy environment will calm him down without the need to feed.

Ready-made formula is another option. While this is usually a more expensive alternative to the powder, all you need to do is pour it into a feeding bottle, so it's just super easy and doesn't involve lots of faffing around making up bottles.

Usually available in 70ml or 200ml sizes, both can be stored in a cupboard until opened. Once opened they must be kept in the fridge and used within a certain time frame. Storage details will be on the packaging.

The 70mls come with their own screw-on teats; they are handy for when your milk has not yet come in, but your baby is hungry and needs to feed little and often, or for topping him up during growth spurts.

You might want to do a combination of both breast and bottle (either formula or expressed breast milk); this is referred to as

Mixed Feeding. In that instance it would make more sense to seek out bottles that replicate the shape of your own breast/nipple more accurately.

Many babies will simply take whatever is given without any fuss, but I've noticed that the length of the actual teat can sometimes be a little challenging for newborns; they may gag if it is a little too long. You may need to try a few different brands until you find one your baby likes. The epitome of *Suck it and See*.

What works for some of your Antenatal Class's Text Message group/other mum friends may not work for you and your baby, so don't be pushed into buying a product just because it suited someone else.

If you are purely bottle feeding, then it is just a matter of trial and error until you find the shape your baby prefers.

As a guide:

When your baby is born their stomach is tiny; they need to feed little and often. The tummy size increases rapidly over the first month and as a result you will notice that the amounts they can take from a bottle will creep up day by day.

To help you visualise their tummy size, see the table on the next page.

DAY	TUMMY SIZE	FEED AMOUNT
One	Cherry	5-7ml/0.1-0.2 oz per feed
Three	Walnut	22-27ml/0.8-1oz per feed
Seven	Apricot	45-60ml/1.5-2oz per feed
Thirty	Egg	80-150ml/2.5-5oz per feed

Some babies will take a little more than this, some a little less. Just like us, their appetites vary; babies tend to feed when they are hungry and stop when full.

Never try to force your baby to feed when they don't want it. I have seen mothers desperately trying to encourage the baby to take the same amount feed after feed, and the end result is usually messy. They overload their stomach and the discomfort that ensues ends up with them jettisoning the whole lot all down your front or they will be overly full and miserable for the next 4 hours.

You may want to buy a bottle steriliser unit, or you may choose to wash your bottles by hand. If you are short of space in your kitchen and have a microwave, there are microwave sterilisers available.

Whilst most of the Western world has now been royally brainwashed by the TV ads, having us all living in fear that bacteria is taking over the world, it should be noted that unless you live somewhere where there is a strong likelihood that the water from your taps may be contaminated, then it is not necessary to sterilise bottles each time you use them; if it is safe enough for you to drink it is safe enough to wash your bottles in.

> *Here's a good article about sterilizing your bottles:*
> https://www.webmd.com/parenting/baby/
> should-you-sterilize-your-babys-bottles

If your baby is poorly, premature or has other medical issues then yes, sterilising is a necessity. If not, you can stand down and wash up. Bacteria is all around you, so you might as well learn to get along.

If you don't quite like that idea, then you can buy some baby bottle baskets and pop the bottles, lids and teats in the dishwasher.

All brand-new bottles and breast pump equipment should be washed and sterilised before the first use. If you are not using a steriliser, put bottles, lids, fastening rings and teats and all non-electrical parts of the pump in a large saucepan of boiling water or drop everything in a bowl of Milton sterilising solution.

Please do your research and make up your own minds about which advice you choose to follow.

You will need:

SMALL PLASTIC WASHING UP BOWL
Also called, The Baby Bowl.

BOTTLE & TEAT BRUSH
This is usually included in any bottle starter kit box.

WATER, WASHING UP LIQUID & A CLEAN TEA TOWEL
You can also use a kitchen roll.

Using the dedicated Baby Bowl, thus avoiding contamination from wayward food debris in your kitchen sink, wash your bottles and any pumping equipment in hot, soapy water and rinse thoroughly before air drying on a clean kitchen towel or kitchen roll.

In the summertime, I immediately dry them by hand and store them in a Tupperware box/designated baby bottle cupboard in case of contamination by flies.

PREPARING AND STORING FORMULA FEEDS

The directions for preparation and storage of powdered formula milk will be written on the side of the packaging/box/tin, but in a nutshell the current guidelines are:

🍼 **BOIL KETTLE**

🍼 **LEAVE FOR 30 MINUTES TO COOL**

🍼 **POUR MEASURED AMOUNT INTO BOTTLE**

🍼 **USING SPOON INSIDE THE FORMULA TIN**
Scoop up powder and level it off using the little tag on the tub rim or the back of a clean knife.

🍼 **ADD REQUIRED NUMBER OF SCOOPS**
You use one scoop per 30ml/1oz water.

SHAKE BOTTLE TO DISSOLVE POWDER

 STAND BOTTLE IN COLD WATER
This brings temperate down to lukewarm.

 FEED BABY

Years ago, the guidelines told us to make up all the required number of bottles of formula for 12 hours or so. We would then store them in the fridge until the feed time and this seemed to work just fine. I would bring down any overnight bottles first thing in the morning, wash, rinse and dry them. Then I would boil the kettle and make up four bottles for the feeds at 6am, 10am 2pm and 5pm.

At 4.30pm I would clean and dry all used bottles and prepare more for 6pm, 10pm 2am and 6am.

The next rule change told us not to do that anymore, and we were instructed to add boiled water to the bottles, leaving them parked on the side in the kitchen, adding the powder as and when needed.

Several years later and yet more new rules apply. Sigh!

My advice? Do a bit of asking around amongst some of your more seasoned mum-friends and make a judgement call.

HOW MUCH AND HOW OFTEN?

Unlike greedy grown-ups, babies tend to be slightly more sensible in their approach to eating. All new mums worry whether their baby is getting enough at each feed to begin with. This is easy to gauge when a baby is bottle fed, but not so when breastfeeding because you can't see your precious milk disappearing before your eyes.

Remember, your baby's stomach is tiny to start with, so don't expect him to be downing pints of the stuff just yet.

•	Day 1	5 ml	per feed
•	Day 2	12-20 ml	per feed
•	Day 3	30-40 ml	per feed
•	Day 6	60-80 ml	per feed

(30 ml = 1oz for bottle measurements)

Day 4-10: You need to feed your baby 3-4 hourly until your baby has regained any weight that was lost following the birth. Your visiting midwives will monitor this until the baby is gaining weight steadily and feeding is going well.

The easiest way to tell that your baby is feeding well is to check the evidence in the nappy. This information may have been given to you in your antenatal classes as a handout and will have full colour pictures for added enjoyment.

I've always thought it looks like one of those rather dodgy

Chinese Restaurant window menus showing the various dishes on offer.

We professionals simply call it The Poo Chart. You can find the full technicolour version by searching this link: www.nct.org.uk/baby-toddler/nappies-and-poo/newborn-baby-poo-nappies-what-expect.

•	Black poos	days 0 - 2
•	Green poos	days 3 - 4
•	Brown poos	days 5 - 6
•	Orangey poos	days 7 - 8
•	Yellowy poos	days 9 - 10
•	Yellow/Mustardy poos	from then on

During these stages, you may notice flecks of dark green spinachy looking bits, white lumps not unlike cottage cheese; even black specks that look like small seeds. Given that all you are putting in one end is milk, it's quite puzzling to see the variety of colours and textures they produce at the other end. This is all perfectly normal and will settle down in a few days.

If the poo is not changing up in colour as per this chart, then it may be that you need to offer your baby more feeds, or if you are only doing one breast per feed, start offering two. e.g. Day 5, poo is still black, you need to offer baby more to eat.

Women with larger breasts might end up giving a baby a full feed from one side, whereas women with smaller breasts may need always to offer both sides. It varies enormously from person to person, so do ask your midwife if you are concerned.

If the poos are going up the colour chart towards the Mustard mark more quickly than listed, then pat yourself on the back and know that he is doing brilliantly! His visits to the scales should tell you all you need to know.

While he is tiny feeds can be a long haul, often taking around an hour to complete. Don't worry about this; as both you and he get the hang of it all over the coming weeks, he will become more efficient at feeding, stronger and better at bringing up wind. As his body grows and the digestive system matures, the process becomes more manageable and quite possibly quicker.

Baby's weight loss after birth

It is normal for your new baby to lose a little weight following the birth. He has been "connected to the mains" for the past nine months, having had a steady flow of nutrition delivered without having to work for it. You must not be alarmed now if there is a little dip in the birth weight once he starts life outside the womb. It is perfectly normal.

Average weight loss in a formula fed baby is considered to be 5%, and that is in the first 5-7 days after birth. Breastfed babies can lose between 7%-10% and most babies, whether formula fed or breastfed, will start to regain any lost birth weight soon after the first week.

If their weight continues to fall then there may be underlying issues such as a poor latch, or not enough milk. As mentioned earlier in the book, they may also have physiological feeding challenges such as tongue-tie, lip tie or a high palate.

Your midwife team will monitor any weight loss, giving you advice and guidance if that loss exceeds 10% of your baby's birth weight. Most babies experience this short-term drop in weight following the birth, so try not to worry about it. They are usually on the up and up by 7-10 days after the birth, and before you know it, those little legs will look like turkey drumsticks, and he will have a double chin.

Your feeding station — Breast & Bottle Feeding

First and foremost, establish a feeding station. Ideally this should be somewhere warm, not too bright and where you can sit with your feet flat on the floor, your lap flat and your back well supported so that you don't slump backwards. Of course, you can feed anywhere you wish, but you may find it helpful to pick a couple of sacred corners. One comfy chair in a kitchen and one in the baby's room perhaps.

Set up a little table beside you with things you need/want to hand. Assemble your mobile phone, a big bottle of water and a glass, biscuits, fruit and a notepad. That will be good to get you up and running. Make sure you have one of the many muslin cloths you bought nearby too. It's quite frustrating when Tiny Small regurgitates some of his feed into your lap but your muslin stash is all still neatly folded in the bottom drawer of the changing table upstairs. These little things can tip you over the edge.

CHAPTER 11

SAFE SLEEP ADVICE

"SWADDLING IS A SKILL THAT NEEDS TO BE PRACTICED. IF A
BABY COMES LOOSE FROM HIS SWADDLE, THEN, SIMPLY PUT,
YOU HAVE NOT GOT IT QUITE RIGHT".

SUDDEN INFANT DEATH SYNDROME (S.I.D.S.)

Thankfully, SIDS is becoming less common now that guidelines are being followed.

It is still important that you keep to these guidelines for prevention.

- Put the baby to sleep on his back.

- Do not smoke; keep the baby out of smoky atmospheres.

- Do not let the baby get too warm (refer to temperature guidelines).

- Put the baby at the foot of the cot so that he cannot wriggle under any covers.

- Contact a doctor if you think the baby is unwell.

- Ensure that you adjust the baby's clothing/coverings according to the room temperature .

- Dress the baby accordingly when you take him out in the pram.

- If it is exceptionally cold or snowy, make sure you have a sheepskin/folded blanket or fleece underneath the pram mattress (or a folded blanket) to prevent baby from chilling from below as well as adequate cover over the top.

- Always put a hat on a newborn when going out with the pram in cooler weather. A light cotton one is fine in spring but a wool or fleece one is better in winter.

Please carefully read the information on the NHS website:
https://www.nhs.uk › Health A to Z ›
Your pregnancy and baby guide

NURSERY TEMPERATURE

Many new parents worry incessantly about whether the room is too hot/too cold or just right. Feeling cold themselves, they assume the room must be chilly. When tired and experiencing hormonal fluctuations, it is normal for new mum to feel shivery; when peeling back a cosy duvet after a stolen afternoon nap even more so. Try to make a mental note to double check the nursery temperature before popping more layers than are necessary onto the baby.

You will be taking your baby outside for walks over the coming weeks, won't you? You simply need to learn how to adjust your little one's bedding/clothing according to the ambient temperature.

MUM'S TIP

Do not overdress the baby. Check clothing layers, bedding layers and the room thermometer until you feel more confident.

Assuming the baby is dressed in a cotton vest, a cotton baby-grow and is wrapped in a light swaddle-cloth muslin with a folded cotton cellular blanket over the top, then 18°C is a safe and comfortable temperature for the average household. If your house is cooler than this, pop another layer/another cellular blanket on whilst he is sleeping. Healthy, full-term babies should not wear a hat when indoors.

Premature or poorly babies will need to be kept warmer and

may even need to wear a little wool hat for a few weeks. Your midwife will advise you on this.

The current guidelines stipulate:

21°C = MAXIMUM
16°C = MINIMUM

Note with humour: The baby will not explode at 22°C, nor turn into an ice lolly at 15 °C, but they do need help to maintain the correct body temperature until they get a bit older. Adjust their clothing, open and close windows a little, add or subtract blankets or types of swaddling materials.

In high summer temperatures, use a fan to cool the room. If you freeze a large (plastic) bottle of water, you can stand this in front of the fan. This tip came from an ex-client who had spent silly money on a very fancy brand of fan, only to find that this was far more effective. £499 vs £1.99. A no-brainer really.

A BABY'S BODY TEMPERATURE

- It is essential for adults to monitor them and adjust their clothing/bedding as necessary.
- Young babies cannot control their own body temperature.
- They cannot shiver nor sweat as we do.

TEMPERATURE AND BEDDING

Your newborn baby will normally be wearing a cotton vest and a cotton baby-grow to sleep in. If the ambient temperature in the baby's room reaches 21°C or higher, you should remove the all-in-one baby-grow and just put baby down in a vest and requisite amount of bedding.

Chubbier babies may need one layer less in hot summers.

ROOM TEMP	°C	°F	Bedding Recommended
TOO WARM	27 24 21	80 75 70	Swaddle only Swaddle + light cotton layer Swaddle + 1 light blanket
JUST RIGHT	18	65	Swaddle + 2 blankets
TOO COOL	15 13 10	60 55 50	Swaddle + 3/4 blankets

A once-folded single blanket counts as two blankets.

For example, on a normal spring day in the UK with the inside temperature @ 18°C, you can put the baby down to sleep swaddled in a muslin square folded in half) and single layer of cotton cellular sheet/blanket over the top. Baby can be wearing a vest and baby-grow.

If you need to check to see if the baby is too warm, slide your index finger around the back of his neck, or place your hand on his bare tummy — if it feels sweaty or clammy then remove a blanket. As long as the baby is not placed in a draught, you can have a window open a little to keep the room aired and to cool it down in the warmer months.

- Swaddling -

New babies are totally dependent on your help. They cannot support their heads very efficiently nor control their limbs, bowels, emotions, temper or mood. They need our help 24 hours a day, 7 days a week.

Their development is gradual. The developing brain will not be in charge of some motor functions until they reach about three months of age. For this reason, swaddling is very useful in helping settle a newborn to sleep.

They may *appear* to occasionally find a thumb or fist to suck or grasp an object. This will be the source of much pride to you as the parents. I hate to burst the bubble, but any such movements are usually a complete fluke and cannot be deliberately repeated. However, I am sure he is very advanced/strong/talented as well!

You can swaddle/half swaddle a baby in a cotton muslin cloth until about 10-14 weeks of age for all sleep times. Some mums continue swaddling longer than that if their baby enjoys it, but once they can use their hands and arms, they want to explore their new skill, so may find swaddling a restrictive frustration.

I have persuaded many parents who, despite their initial protestations about their baby apparently "fighting it" or being "so strong that he escapes" etc. went on to become proficient swaddlers. Their babies went to sleep more readily, slept longer and with fewer wakeful moments than those who did not.

The methods I use to swaddle ensure that the arms are controlled (preventing the baby bashing or scratching themselves in the face) but the pelvis and legs are swathed in the looser end of the fabric. This allows the baby to move their legs freely or to generally have a little "wiggle an' a squiggle" before drifting off to sleep. Their hips are not bound; their legs are not pulled straight but fall outward like a spatchcocked chicken.

Swaddling is a skill that needs to be practiced. If a baby comes loose from his swaddle, then, simply put, you have not got it quite right. You may excuse yourselves by believing him to be super strong, highly advanced or talented if that makes you feel better. (But keep practicing).

If you are not sure about how to swaddle your baby, there are plenty of tutorials to be found on-line. Try out a few until you find one that your baby likes.

Do not cover their head. Do not pull their legs straight. Do not restrict their leg movement.

When handling your new baby, you must always support their head. It must not be allowed to flop backwards. It's not going to fall off, but it startles them and is probably rather uncomfortable. Make sure that you always have a hand, or at least a finger, held up to prevent a newborn from flinging his head backwards.

When picking him up you may find it easier to bend over, scooping him into your shoulder as you do so, returning your own body to an upright position. By doing this you will avoid bopping the baby's face onto your shoulder from a standing position. Once his neck muscles begin to develop in a few weeks, his wobbly little head will become more stable.

Babies are quite robust on many levels. Despite your nervousness in the early days, as your confidence grows you will feel more at ease handling your baby. He will mirror you by becoming more relaxed too.

If you have a baby who really doesn't enjoy the swaddle, then you may find that a baby sleeping bag is an option.

As one of the issues with 0-12-week-old babies is the constant flailing of their arms, an unswaddled baby can find settling and staying settled a challenge. Those little flapping arms will constantly bop their faces, waking them up more frequently.

A half-way house could be a sleeping bag which keeps the arms gently contained in a "Take me to your Leader" or "Cactus" pose. Have a skoosh around on Amazon and you'll find something.

Depending on the time of year your baby was born, you will need to buy a sleeping bag of suitable Tog rating to accommodate the weather.

In the UK, tempting though it is to use the opportunity to poke fun at our weather, the summers have been blisteringly hot over the past few years so here are some guidelines for tog ratings:

- Summer: 3.5 - 7.5
- Spring To Autumn: 7.5 - 10.5
- Winter: 15.5 - 15

CHAPTER 12

Dr Jekyll & Mrs Hyde

"It's no surprise that babies, as they develop both
mentally and physically, throw you a new leap
to deal with on an almost weekly basis".

Overwhelm

In preparation for childbirth, your body will have been through many different changes as it produces a variety of hormones. These hormones will physically change your body and can also make themselves felt with an impact on an emotional level.

That's right. Just as you thought you could kick back a bit, you'll realise you are probably going to be off-balance for a little longer.

Once you have safely delivered your baby, you may be happy and tearful all at the same time. These dramatic mood swings may leave you feeling confused, tired and a bit off-kilter. In the space of one hour, you can find yourself chatting away feeling completely normal, only to burst into uncontrollable sobs for no logical reason. Your partner forgot to pick up some milk this morning, or someone asked you what you wanted for lunch, and you become a weeping wreck for no apparent reason. You can feel wildly sensitive to the most innocent of remarks, irritable and unreasonable about trivial matters and impatient with those close to you.

Many mothers feel primed to expect the homecoming to be magical. If reality falls short, they can experience a tremendous sense of disappointment. In fact, new mums experience a considerable dip after a few days. This is known as the Baby Blues and is a perfectly normal part of the big picture. The Baby Blues usually only last from around Day 3 till Day 10.

These mood changes are mainly the result of postpartum hormonal swings, so rest assured that what you are going through is a phase and will pass.

By the way, about phases. Just so you know, every single day/week/month/year with a baby (then a toddler) has phases …

Rather like false horizons … the ones you get on long hikes that your husband makes you take up Mount Snowdon … in horizontal rain … in late October because it's what **he** wanted to do on his birthday …. Hmm? What? Oh, sorry — I went a bit off-piste there, didn't I?

Where was I? Ah yes, false horizons. Just as you feel you have reached the summit; you see another in front of you, and sag with despondency. Take a deep breath and keep telling yourself, "I've **got** this".

It's no surprise that babies, as they develop both mentally and physically, throw you a new leap to deal with on an almost weekly basis. You will eventually learn that there are only pockets of respite where you can draw breath before the next shit storm comes along. Enjoy the pockets and lean forward into the shit storms, and you will do fine.

- How does birth affect my hormones? -

Your body produces many different hormones to help with the birth process and to maintain balance during the pregnancy. It may well take a while yet for those hormones to return to normal now you are home.

Relaxin is secreted by a woman's ovaries, placenta and uterine lining throughout the pregnancy. Its purpose is to inhibit muscle contractions during the pregnancy, so preventing premature birth. At the end of the pregnancy it springs into action to soften and relax the cervix, vagina, ligaments of the pelvis and the membrane around your baby.

As this hormone takes a while to return to normal levels (up to 5 months), many women find they become more prone to muscle sprains. It is essential to be extra careful not to overdo physical activity until you feel more like your old self.

Prolactin is produced to stimulate milk production; this remains active in your body from pregnancy until you cease breastfeeding.

Oxytocin is another hormone that has a significant part to play during labour and again with breastfeeding. By stimulating the uterine muscles to contract as you feed, it facilitates the flow of milk to the breast.

Although all women produce these hormones on their journey through pregnancy and delivery, they are not all *affected* by them in precisely the same way.

These ups and downs of postnatal hormonal swings will gradually settle down by around 6-8 weeks.

- What is a hormonal imbalance? -

In a nutshell. In the morning you feel in control, calm and relatively relaxed given that you are not getting much sleep. Come the afternoon, hormones go on the rampage and you become tearful, overwhelmed and irrational. Babies pick up on this and, in response to the vibe, can become irritable and unsettled thus exacerbating the feeling.

By the time most women reach the six-week mark, they are beginning to feel a little more balanced. They may not have managed being able to shave both legs in one sitting, nor drink a whole cup of tea since getting home, but normality seems to be returning.

By eight weeks in, you might be able to nail having breakfast, lunch and dinner within roughly the same time frame as you did before you had a baby.

This time frame, for those of you who worked a 9-5 style job pre-baby, starts off well with breakfast hoofed down between 6.30-7.30am. Lunch lands between 12.30-2pm (or 11am-5pm if you worked in London's financial square mile). Dinner around 8pm (or 10pm if you had drinks after work ... or not at all if you had a really long lunch in the square mile).

Yet if your hormone levels are still going a bit berserk, you may not feel quite as in control. For some mums, the baby blues experience may drag on longer than average; this could be an indication that there may be a hormone imbalance.

If you think this sounds familiar or are concerned that you may fall into this category, you must discuss this with your partner. Then talk things over with your health visitor, GP or consultant.

There is certainly no shame in feeling that you are "not managing" or coping as well as you thought you might. Sometimes enlisting some practical help may be all it takes to help you on your way. Household chores are not a priority, your baby is. However, you need to eat, shower, do the shopping and get out of the house from time to time.

In the morning you feel in control. Come the afternoon ...

Here are some ideas:

🧒 Ask some friends to cobble together some evening meals for the freezer so you can spend time with your partner at the end of the day.

🧒 Have someone watch the baby for an hour (while he is napping) so that you can have a nice long bath with candles, but this time without staring at the baby monitor which you've balanced on the loo! (FYI: when home alone, it's perfectly fine to have a shower while your baby is asleep in his bed, or he can be happily gawping at you from his bouncy chair on the other side of the glass!).

🧒 Take up the offer from a doting grandmother to spend a couple of hours at home with their beloved grandchild; you can wander down to the high street and join a mate for coffee or just get out for a walk.

🧒 Go for a stroll in your local park and sit on a bench. Read a newspaper in the sun while your partner does a shift at home with the baby.

🧒 If you don't already have one, treat yourself to a two-month contract with a cleaner. She/he can whizz around with a hoover, flick around with the duster and perhaps tidy away the piles of laundry for a few weeks. Maybe you have a friend or neighbour who would be willing to share their cleaner with you for a little while.

♣ Subscribe to one of those DIY Meal Kit Delivery companies for 6 weeks. You know, the ones who send you one clove of garlic, one chicken breast, a knob of butter and some breadcrumbs along with a recipe for Chicken Kiev. Easy!

All the above will go a long way to making you feel a little more human and a little less trapped in a somewhat repetitive day in your own home. As lovely as babies are, they are a bit of a one-way street when it comes to current affairs or heated debates.

You need to stay sane and guilt-free by admitting (perhaps after 2-3 weeks of cooing) that a day at home with a baby can be tedious and trying at times. My clients have said it, so I feel entirely at ease with putting that out there. It's not that they don't love them, but it's easy to feel frustrated with the same-old, same-old day after day.

People approach you for weeks saying things like, "Are you loving it?", or "Are you enjoying your maternity leave?". Well, in all honestly, most of my clients have responded pretty well when asked this. The polite and PC response of course, "Yes. It's tiring but wonderful."

What they actually *want* to say is, "Not really, no. But since you ask, my days are pretty much totally shit on a stick from dawn till dusk, I haven't had time to bathe for a week and smell like a dustbin, my husband is crap and behaves as though the two weeks of paternity leave is all that is required of him, we have fought more in the past two weeks than in the whole of our relationship and now he has gone back to work and thinks I spend all day watching Love Island and having chats with my antenatal group and I am already longing to go back to work so I can drink a hot cup of coffee and have breakfast before midday. But thanks for asking. Oh, and by the way, I love my baby to the moon and back and would totally walk naked through a trench of alligators if he needed me to."

I have re-visited my Mums months, or even years after my time with them. They all describe those first few weeks as a "fog".

They can vaguely remember the sensation of many formless and sleep shattered nights melting into equally chaotic and unpredictable days. They felt glued to their nursing chairs as the sun rose and set again, feeling they had hardly moved. If the baby had had a bad day, they were still in their PJs come 5pm, realising they had skipped not only breakfast and lunch, but a morning wash too.

The temporary chaos that a new baby brings to your world has to be experienced to be believed, but little by little you will adapt and so will your baby.

An uneasy truce seems to be reached by the end of Week Eight when you both end up panting, eyeing each other from opposite corners of the metaphorical boxing ring.

At this point, you acknowledge that neither one of you is perfect, nor will either of you be an outright winner. You shake hands, hug it out and then turn to face into the shit storm that is the next round (sorry, phase) together.

Miraculously, all my lovely mums are all still here; even more miraculously, still smiling. They have come through the fog and have crossed over to the other side.

Postnatal depression

If you feel overwhelmed at the very thought of another day. If you have trouble sleeping (above and beyond the normal night waking required to feed your baby); if you find it hard to stay asleep because you continually analyse every peep your baby makes, then you may need medical help.

If you feel depressed most of the time, and this feeling does not go away, speak to your doctor.

It is normal for a new mother to show a certain amount of concern about her baby. But being overly anxious *all the time*, perhaps filled with dread in the early hours about the day to come, is not normal. Even if that day is nothing too dramatic, then you must talk about this with those close to you, your partner and most definitely your GP/health visitor.

- Postnatal Depression (PND) affects about one in every ten mums in the UK.
- Onset is usually within the first 4-6 weeks after birth
- Sometimes it develops over several months
- It is not just caused by hormonal changes
- It does not go away on its own
- It is treatable

Hormonal imbalance treatments are available; there is a process to help ascertain what type of help is needed. Please don't feel that you must suffer in silence or that it is anything to be ashamed about. No-one is going to judge you and, once the correct treatments are sorted out, you will feel like a new woman. You'll pass this way but once as a first-time mum, so please seek help if you think you are not coping. You can then enjoy the time you have with your new baby without dragging that little black rain cloud around over your head.

- Emily's story -

Many years ago, I worked with Emily (name changed for privacy purposes) a first-time mum who spent every second between feeds, her baby sleeping soundly in his crib, worrying about the next bit of the day. She described how she woke at 3-4am every morning, feeling physically sick about the day ahead, filled with fear and dread. Her in-laws had arranged a cleaning company to help her out for a few weeks and her husband organised food and evening meals.

She did nothing; nothing but stand in her spotlessly clean kitchen pulling at her cuticles or twiddling her hair. Meanwhile, her baby woke every 3.5hrs for feeds, played happily between naps and went to sleep without any trouble.

Every day she was overcome with tension and misery. We discussed getting her some help and the next day made an appointment to see the GP. Within a few days, an assessment had been carried out. Professional counselling was put in place and they arranged to put her on a course of tablets to kick her hormones back into shape. After a couple of trials, they found ones that suited her.

After it was all over, she wrote about how she'd felt in her darkest moments so that other mums might see that they are not alone.

"I hated every moment of my day. I felt as though I was standing in a small, dark room while my baby lurked somewhere in the shadows, sleeping yet just waiting for me to do something wrong; to misread him or hurt him in some way, by mistake.

I couldn't bear to pick him up because I felt as though he would sense that I didn't love him; that I didn't want to be a mother after all. I hated myself and I didn't bond with him. I loved him, but I didn't ... does that makes sense?

Everyone else seemed elated, proud and happy. Yet I felt like a complete fraud. I didn't have any of those feelings, so I simply pretended to be happy, telling everyone I was fine. I even lied to the midwives and health visitor when they asked how I was coping, so they ticked their boxes and signed me off. It was easy to put on a front. I felt so guilty, but I couldn't admit it to anyone.

Over the next three weeks, everyone began to become concerned as my façade began to crack. My husband was confused because I certainly was not the calm, collected and reliable woman he married. He was due to return to work but was deeply scared of leaving me alone. I felt locked away in my own head, terrified that if I admitted how I was feeling that someone would take my baby away from me. That I would be judged as a terrible mother.

I had failed. I was never going to get the hang of this new role, this new life as a parent.

He contacted Hattie and explained his concerns about leaving me alone and it was arranged that she would come for a few days whilst he was at work.

He told me that she was just coming to give me some coaching and, although I wasn't wild about the idea, I had to go along with it to keep up the pretence.

With Hattie's experience, it didn't take long for her to see that things were not as they seemed. She was incredibly tactful and gently drew me out about how I was feeling. Gradually I began to speak about how I felt, and Hattie then gently steered the situation, persuading me to contact my GP and Health Visitor.

Far from the judgment I was expecting, they reassured me, explaining the process and a proper PND screening was arranged. Asking all the right questions to see where I was on the PND scale, they began offering suggestions for treatment and wheels began to turn. Just being able to verbalise how I was feeling in a safe place was a relief in itself.

It wasn't a quick fix. It took a couple weeks and subsequent trials to find the right medication/dosage that worked for me. Once it did, it was, honestly, like the sun coming out. I felt as though someone had walked into that dark room and thrown open the curtains. I experienced a surge of love and acceptance towards my baby boy. Overwhelmed with relief that I was going to be a good mum and have thoroughly enjoyed him since. There were still challenging days ahead, but that is part of life as mother. When your head is straight and you love your baby, you will cope, even when they drive you potty!"

- Postnatal psychosis -

Postnatal psychosis is a severe form of depression, although quite rare. It develops in about one in 1,000 mothers. Amongst other symptoms, a mother may experience irrational behaviour, confusion and suicidal thoughts. Women with postnatal psychosis often need specialist psychiatric treatment.

One woman's personal experience of, and recovery from, Postnatal Psychosis following the birth of her son can be read in the incredible book "Eyes without Sparkle" by Elaine Hanzak. I have had the pleasure of spending time with Elaine on several occasions. This smiling, petite lass is a giant amongst women.

- Bonding with your baby -

Bonding normally begins as soon as your baby is born. If it has been possible for you to have immediate skin to skin contact with him within minutes of his arrival, that is great. Sometimes there are other priorities at that precise moment. If he has been whisked away from you for medical attention then don't worry, the bond will not be broken; you can focus on it when you are both in a better position to do so.

If the birth has been quite straightforward and you are comfortable enough for your baby to be handed to you, you may find that he snuffles around, finding your nipple quickly and begins to feed. Some babies get it, some babies don't so just go with the flow and enjoy holding him close. If you are feeling a bit battered, he can be given to your partner. It is important for both caregivers to have this experience.

Your baby may be quite alert following the birth and want to lie in your arms, staring up at your face. Just allow him time to do this as he works out who you are. Looking into the eyes of your new baby is a great way to bond. It is proven that doing this strengthens the neural synchronization between baby and adult.

During the first 2-3 weeks or so, you may find that you don't get many opportunities to just look at your baby. He will have his eyes shut much of the time, even when feeding; but as your little one wakes up to the world and becomes better equipped to deal with external stimulation, these long lingering looks will be part of your day.

Over the coming weeks, baby bonding is about so much more than just doing skin-to-skin time and baby gazing. Feeding, holding, playing, nappy changes and bathing become very intimate and special moments for you to further strengthen this bond.

Please note: some mothers find it takes a while to feel that connection and everyone's experience is different, so try to be patient while you get to know each other. We all hear about the surge of love, or a magically bonding moment when a mum first meets her new baby, but for many, that moment comes much further down the line. Give it time.

www. HowToBecomeNeurotic.com

My time spent working with newborns began almost a quarter of a century ago, in a time when we sought wisdom and guidance from reliable and trusted sources and close friends.

Now we are addicted to our technological devices and shuffle around like Quasimodo, hunched over mobile phones as if our very lives depended on them.

Back in the good old days, when new mums were surrounded with a bevy of experienced females for support, most would have been able to seek advice from their mothers, aunts and grandmothers or other mums within their close personal circle.

Those that didn't have that luxury just had to knuckle down and get on with it. It would have been a tough and lonely existence, but mostly they coped.

During the past few years, I have seen first-hand how negatively the arrival of the internet has impacted on the confidence of my clients.

Where previously a first-time mum would have been visited on a daily basis by an NHS midwife, now they are lucky if they get more than two appointments in a week; many less than that, often having to make their way to their nearest Baby Clinic days at their local GP Surgery for guidance or reassurance.

Once fathers have had to return to work and the ebb and flow of clucking, eager visitors has slowed to a trickle, new mums can suddenly feel massively isolated and trapped at home.

Still sore from the delivery perhaps, anxious at facing the days without much in the way of company, cabin fever can set in. Feeding a baby every 2-3 hours day may begin to feel very repetitive, yet the prospect of venturing out of the house in the early days is very daunting when you are on your own.

Coupled with the lack of access to family or friends with children of their own, mothers (and fathers) resort to harvesting information from the internet, believing every scare-mongering word they read.

Before they truly tap into their instincts, feeling anxious that they may be "doing things wrong", they disappear into the depths of their laptops, burrowing into hundreds of sites for baby advice.

They surface hours later, wild eyed and brainwashed, having gorged on a variety of poorly researched articles, feeling even more confused and concerned. Any sensible advice previously given by reliable and trustworthy people is shunned and newly planted fears bubble to the surface..

A brand new, still embryonic hysteria is thus born.

By the time the Text Message group get hold of it, they will believe it with the same ferocity as the "Elvis is Alive" brigade.

And no, he isn't! But if you know otherwise, please tell me because I remember the moment my mother told me about his death on 16th August 1977 and, as a massive fan, I was pretty cut up about it. If he is still uh-huhing somewhere out there, letters will be written, mark my words!

You can find whatever answer you want on the internet (including sightings of Elvis). I highlighted this to some of my clients recently while casually looking at the crime statistics in an area where we were house hunting.

For the same country lane, same village, same county, even

for the same year, a website listed the address as having both the highest *and* lowest crime rates in the area simultaneously. As if that wasn't daft enough, get this. That little gem I gleaned from precisely the same source; one statistic being listed immediately under the other.

It is worth noting that many articles, particularly when it comes to emotive issues such as parenting or babies, are opinion based and therefore have little or no basis in fact.

Theories, perhaps and personal feelings for sure — but not fact.

When challenged by someone starting a sentence with, "I read somewhere that ...", or "...but there was this mum on a forum who said ...", going on to quote a snippet of some flimsy bit of inflammatory misinformation, I have always responded to with the following question:

"Would you write out a question about your baby on a billboard, march through Paddington Station with it held above your head and then act on the advice of the first twenty-five total strangers who walk up to you?"

The answer of course is, "No, of course, not".

In essence, without further investigation into the authenticity of that piece of information, I fail to see how looking up *stuff* on the internet or giving it any more credence, differs from the Paddington Station approach.

My advice about the use of the internet for finding out about your baby, or anything else for that matter is:

1. Actively seek out websites from reputable institutions, such as research centres, universities, well know associations and hospitals.

2. Think about what the purpose of each site is. Is someone trying to sell you a product or asking you to give your

opinion (clickbait/accumulation of Likes), or fuel a self-serving public debate to perhaps promote a contentious book/TV show/product, or are they merely giving their personal opinion?

3. Be wary of sites that present biased information or come from unprofessional backgrounds. Take commercial sites with a big pinch of salt or avoid them altogether.

4. Find out how current the information is. Remember that medical research, in particular, is always being updated and revised.

5. Always dig deeper! Check to see who carried out the research, how authentic were the results, what proof they have to support their reports.

Open a file and save articles or research from trusted sources so that you have it available as and when you need it.

It is worth holding this bit of advice in your head:
If there is "conflicting advice" about a topic, then it is not yet fact. It is still just a theory or an opinion.

You do not have to agree with the theories or opinions of others until they are proven to be factual, when until proved otherwise, are indisputable.

You can have your own opinion while still respecting that others have theirs too.

CHAPTER 13

THE NAPPY FORECAST

"MOST BABIES ARRIVE WITH LOVELY SKIN. THEY ARE SMOTHERED IN A GREASY LAYER KNOWN AS VERNIX. IT IS NATURE'S VERY OWN MOISTURISER, AND THIS WILL KEEP THEM BEAUTIFULLY SOFT FOR A LITTLE WHILE YET".

Welcome to the world of poo. I don't mean the famously cute yellow teddy bear with his little furry friends, but the frequent, colourful, explosive and often unbelievably huge quantities produced by your oh-so-adorable Tiny Small.

You will, despite your best efforts, be drawn into that dark place where new parents dwell in the early days; the place where you talk about poo in the same way you used to chat about the weather, or the latest binge watch on Netflix. Poo will become a focus for a while, and you will compare notes/photos and even quantities with others in your inner baby circle.

Why? Because poo is a great indicator of your baby's overall state of health, so it is only natural that you become more than a little obsessed by it.

Too dark and he's not getting enough to eat, too green and he may not be getting enough hind milk, too thick and he may be dehydrated.

The list goes on, but before we go deeper into poo (not a pleasant thought), let's chat about how to clean the stuff off the little stinkers.

As mentioned elsewhere in this book, I believe in being prepared for battle, so before I embark upon most things with my babies, I make sure I have my front line in place. The area where you have your changing table, nappies, creams, spare clothes etc. is generally referred to as The Changing Station.

You are going to have to really develop a sense of humour about now. There is no way of avoiding nappy changing. You can choose your camp on most topics, but nappies are nappies and poo just keeps on coming!

Try to make sure you have a good size changing table and not one that simply houses a standard sized changing mat and a very small day-old baby. They grow … and they muck spread like you wouldn't believe! Have you ever seen the David Attenborough programme with the pooping hippos? Well, watch and learn!

To prepare you, I suggest that you get a new bottle of tomato ketchup in a squeezy bottle, go into the garden, lay it on the lawn and stamp on it. Hard! Now — that just about replicates the phenomenal distance a projectile poo could travel. You have been warned.

Quickly now! Head back into the nursery and remove the grinning menagerie of pastel coloured innocents: the ducklings, teddies, dolls and bunnies parked in the projectile poo flight path.

Great Aunty Gwen's hand-me-down … the *totally*-not-BSS-kite-marked, no-eyed, one-eared grinning beast of our nightmares, which was once (with a huge stretch of the imagination) a well-loved teddy bear could probably stay. It will die a horrible death eventually, and probably not before its time!

At least this takes it permanently out of the gene pool, and you won't contemplate handing it down to the next unfortunate generation in your family.

A sneeze mid-wipe can fire out poo at supersonic speeds, leaving a skid mark worthy of entry into the Guinness Book of Records. Travelling right across your beige carpet, hitting everything in its path until it reaches the finish line.

There it will slide slowly down the newly decorated nursery wall like an expression falling off a face upon opening a really disappointing Christmas present.

Put up a cricket screen behind you. And buy a splat mat to put on the floor to protect the carpet … you can use it again under the highchair when your baby moves onto solid food.

If you can choose a category for each type of nappy change, it can help to highlight the severity when you shriek into the monitor for assistance from your partner.

Tornado & Severe Storm: a poo that has been ejected at speed with force from a following wind and the contents now reach both this neck and his ankles. You are going to have to cut the clothing off him and head straight to the bathroom for this one. Full on Emergency Service support needed.

Hurricane & Tropical Storm: Halfway through the change he decided to shoot out another couple of litres, and you are now holding him aloft by his ankles like a piping bag on Bake Off. Help required urgently.

Floods: He waited until he was lying on the plastic mat without a towel under him before he had a poo and pee simultaneously and is now sliding around in a brown swamp. Send in the military.

A sneeze mid-wipe can fire out poo at supersonic speeds

Earthquakes: Having legged it up the stairs three at a time with the baby held out at arm's length, on opening the nappy there is nothing there but the last wiffs of a really bad fart. Apologise for wasting everyone's time and turn off the alarms.

Drought: Sounded like a poo. Smelled like a poo. Baby's face looked as though he was definitely doing a poo, but there is absolutely nothing to show for it. All Military personnel on call can stand down.

Inventory reminders before battle commences ... on the changing station top deck, you should have:

OLD TOWEL OR MAT COVER

BABY BALM

TISSUES

SMALL BASKET OR BOWL

PLEATED COTTON WOOL OR LARGE MAKE-UP REMOVER PADS

2 X SMALL PLASTIC BOWLS OF WATER/DOUBLE TOP 'N' TAIL BOWL

ANTI-BACTERIAL HAND GEL

🚼 Muslin cloth

In the drawers/shelves immediately underneath the top deck:

🚼 Stacks of nappies

🚼 Vests

🚼 Baby-Grows

🚼 More muslin cloths

🚼 Nappy rash cream

Near the changing table, no more than arm's length away: a Nappy Disposal Unit or similar vessel to put the soiled nappies in.

You will probably have been shown basic nappy changing skills whilst in hospital, but in case you have little experience of such joys, then these tips may help.

Make sure that the changing mat is covered with an old towel. Babies all seem to do what I call a *Wake Up Wee Wee* within moments of you removing the old nappy from under them. If you are blessed with a little girl, this is a quiet and almost genteel moment, like a little water feature tinkling away. If they are lying on a plastic cover, it will quickly spread right up their backs and a simple nappy change instantly escalates into a full strip down, body wash and re-dress. No fun at the 3 am feed!

Little boys, who seem to have a lifelong need to wave their willies around whenever they get the chance, pee straight up into the air.

If you, your face, pictures on the wall or your Operation Nappy Change wing- man/woman happen to be in the line of fire — you can look on it as being lucky (if that gets you through) and quickly pounce on it with a tissue to prevent a thorough soaking.

Once you no longer find this quite as amusing as you did the first week, you will probably learn to have the tissue poised and to wait a few minutes after opening the nappy whilst keeping the front of the nappy vertical.

Occasionally they pee all over their own faces, so then and only then do you get to do a little "I told you so" dance and have laugh at their expense. Their expression, always one of complete disbelief, is one of those moments that keeps you going and makes you giggle. Wipe them down and crack on.

As a preventative measure against nappy leakage with boys, if you smear a little barrier cream on his scrotum, then stick his willie (pointing downwards), there is less likelihood of him spraying pee out of the top of the nappy.

Make sure there is always a stash of clean nappies/muslins/clothes at the ready in the top drawer. You want to avoid the hassle of getting the baby to the naked stage before realizing that everything is downstairs/in the wash/still on order from Ocado.

Let Battle Commence!

⇒ Pop baby on the mat.

⇒ Plonk two or three chunks of cotton wool into the water.

⇒ Open up the baby-grow by undoing the poppers at the crotch and pull up to baby's chest level. Fact of life: there are always two more poppers than pop holes when you come to do it back up. It's not important! No-one is going to check on your performance.

⇒ See if you can master trapping his arms across his chest by pulling the clothing over them. Like a little straight jacket! This will avoid fingers finding nappy contents and covering themselves with whatever they unearth down there.

⇒ Peel back the sticky tabs on the front of the nappy and fold them back on themselves so that they don't re-attach to the baby's skin, your skin, the mat, the cotton wool, his clothes or the tissue.

⇒ Gently open nappy (without removing it completely) and examine the fallout.

⇒ If brown, add more cotton wool to the bowl and get a disposable nappy sack in place off to the side, with the opening wide to accommodate the incoming brown article.

⇒ If just wet, do a small dance of joy.

⇒ In both cases, tentatively hold the front of the nappy slightly ajar, allowing a slight breeze to hit his nether regions. Normally within 2 minutes, he will do a Wake-Up Wee Wee.

⇒ Baby boys will require you leap into action by closing the front of the nappy in self-defence till they finish and the older they get, the funnier they think this party trick becomes. But you're not a real parent till you've been peed on in this way. Baby girls do a rather less dramatic trickle and sigh. In both instances, the baby will often quite suddenly calm just before they pee, so you may become an expert pee forecaster.

⇒ Once the danger has passed, you can set about the clear up.

⇒ You may like to simply drop the pieces of dirty cotton wool into the nappy as you go, removing it at the end, but I normally risk it and remove the nappy completely to make cleaning easier. Occasionally the baby throws a surprise poo out, but that's part of the fun!

⇒ Little girls must be wiped from front to back to avoid any bacteria entering the vagina which may cause infection. With **clean** fingers, gently separate her vaginal lips and wipe with moistened cotton wool. There is usually a layer of discharge which looks a little like egg white; this is natural and is her natural protection. You do not have to clean this away, although if a poo has travelled up to the front of her nappy, then a clean-up is called for.

⇒ Little boys can be generally wiped clean by using dampened cotton wool and cleaning around the penis and scrotum — there is no need to pull back the skin on the penis

Slide a clean nappy under your baby's bottom whilst you do the final wipe over, then pat them dry with either a tissue or a cotton muslin cloth before removing the top nappy to reveal the nice clean one underneath. It's about now that they decide to do just a tiny bit more pooping. That's life!

Once the explosive areas are contained, re-clothe the baby and then you can carry on with your feed or settle baby down to sleep.

TOP & TAILING

Top & Tailing is a usually carried out once a day.

I suggest doing this mid-morning, at around 9-10am which helps to establish a nice little "Start of Day" ritual. After all, we will do a similar process when they are toddlers, so lay down good habits early on.

Top Tip: Feed your baby *before* you start Top & Tail cleaning.

As tiny babies are pretty shouty about almost every element of changing/washing/bathing to start with, I find that it's a much nicer experience all round if they are either completely fed, or at the very least have had Starter and Main Course before embarking on a full body wash.

If you have remembered to include a little basket/bowl with lumps of cotton wool or make-up remover pads on your changing mat, then put a few into the bowl of water now.

Having completed the nappy change, remove the baby's vest and baby-grow. It helps if the room is nice and warm for this process. Slide your arm under his neck so that his head gently falls backwards, giving you better access to those chubby little crevasses under his chin and swiftly clean with cotton wool.

Milky dribbles and occasional possets can collect in these little places and if left unchecked will result in your Tiny Small becoming a Tiny Smell ... not unlike a particularly good vintage of Mont D'or cheese. Throw the cotton wool wodge away immediately when you have finished that bit.

Newborns don't relish having their necks or their armpits cleaned, but unfortunately, it's non-negotiable, so you may have to brace yourself for a bit of a grump-fest for a few minutes. I prefer getting the neck and armpits out of the way before doing the less challenging areas, but it's your call.

Take a fresh piece of wet cotton wool for each area. You don't want to be wiping their face with the same piece of cotton wool with which you have done their armpits!

The armpits can end up being quite stinky if left unsupervised. Fluff from their clothing coupled with sweat and shedding skin makes for a potent cocktail, so make sure that you lift their arms in a proper air-punch pose, gently using your fingers to stretch out their underarm skin to give you full access and give it a good wipe.

If you have neglected this area in fear of the shouty bit, then you will soon see that it can quickly build a white, smelly deposit. If left to fester, this can cause skin irritations not dissimilar to nappy rash. In that situation, clean and dry the area well and apply a light layer of nappy rash cream until the skin calms down.

You can then progress to clean behind his ears, around the back of his neck, behind his knees, palms of his hands and between his toes. If you have a lovely chubby baby, you will need to delve into any little areas where there are folds of flesh to make sure it is spring cleaned on a daily basis.

Once you have a sparkling Tiny Small, you can re-dress him and continue with your day.

Even when you are bathing your baby several times each week, the Top & Tail process should be done every morning.

Your Tiny Small becomes a Tiny Smell.

- Cord care -

When your baby's umbilical cord is cut, they will crimp it with a little plastic clip much like those we use on freezer bags. This and the little remnant of the umbilical it is clipped to is what midwives refer to as *The Cord*. Both the clip and the cord stump to which it is attached, remain on for about 8-10 days before falling off on their own as the stump dries and shrivels up. It does not look particularly pretty but rest assured that a nice neat little tummy button will appear eventually.

In the meantime, there is no need to worry about it. It does not cause the baby any pain, even though it looks wet and a bit bloody to start with. It is advisable to avoid bathing the baby until the cord has dropped off.

Meanwhile, you simply need to keep an eye on it, making sure that the stump and the area around it are kept clean and dry, avoiding using cotton wool here; fibres can get caught in the sticky area around the base of the stump which may lead to inflammation or infection.

When fastening a nappy when the cord is still in place, make sure that you leave it a little loose around the waistband, turning the top down a fraction so that it does not get pulled around too much. Again, although it may make you feel a bit squeamish, it does not hurt the baby at all.

If the stump begins to appear red or the surrounding skin becomes inflamed, call your midwife and ask them to take a look. It may need a little attention with some antiseptic wipes, but better to ask for a professional opinion in case it is infected. If you pay attention to the area, keeping it clean and dry, this can be avoided.

Once the cord drops off, the belly button can be cleaned with a soft cloth and warm water. Over the following few days, the last of the dried blood will fall away to reveal a perfect Innie or Outie! His little tummy will fatten up over the coming weeks and months, so even the proudest Outie may retreat and become an Innie eventually!

SKIN CARE

Most babies arrive with lovely skin. They are smothered in a greasy layer known as vernix. It is nature's very own moisturiser, and this will keep them beautifully soft for a little while yet.

Personally, I advise against bathing a baby too often. Some babies seem to be prone to skin problems such as eczema or cradle cap, so perhaps less is more. The water in London is particularly hard, so if your own water supply errs on the hard side and you notice your baby's skin starting to develop dry patches, perhaps reduce the number of weekly baths.

As you are going to be Top & Tailing your baby on a daily basis, bathing them more than 3 times a week is not necessary, but some people like to incorporate it as part of their bedtime routine. If your baby is particularly prone to dry skin or has other dermatological issues, then perhaps leave nightly bathing until they are a little older.

Creams which contain organic and natural products have to be the top of my list. I've always felt that if I cannot pronounce the long names of the ingredients on the back of the tub, then it is probably better not to put it on the baby's skin.

I bet you've been wondering why I suggested Jumbo Porridge Oats in my shopping list. Well, here it is.

For bath times, I simply use a handful of porridge oats popped in a little square of cut muslin tied with a bit of string and dropped into the bathwater before bathing the baby. Like a tea bag. You could also buy a pack of pop-sox from your local department store or cut the foot off an old pair of tights and use that instead. This has done the trick for me for many years.

Once it has soaked in the bathwater for a few minutes, give it a good squeeze (the porridge pouch, not the baby) and it will exude a lovely cloud of milky goodness which will result in skin as soft as … you guessed it … a baby's bottom!

Once your baby is older, you might like to start using a good quality organic baby shampoo or in-bath product.

After baths in the evening, it is nice to give your baby a little all over massage using something very plain such as organic coconut or almond oil.

FINGERS AND TOES

Toenails seem to take care of themselves. In 25 years, I have not once had to cut a tiny baby's toenails. I assume they just rub away inside the feet of the baby-grows. A mystery. However, if you notice your little one has small claws appearing on the end of his feet, or scratch marks on the foot of the cot, then break out the manicure kit when he is snoozing and give him a pedicure.

Fingernails are a different story. They grow at a rate of knots and babies seem hell bent on scratching and gouging their faces as a pastime whenever they get the chance.

In the early months a baby will naturally scrunch up their fists, so daily manicures can be challenging. Like trying to shuck an oyster, baby's hands are far from co-operative. I tend to wait until they are either milk-drunk (when you can get away with practically anything) or asleep, in which case it's like tip toeing across a floor covered with mousetraps. You know the risks, and if you rouse the sleeping beast all hell may break loose.

Very fine textured nail files can be found on Amazon or in good chemists. The rather harsher files used by adults (or on gels/ acrylics) is too aggressive for your baby's much softer nails. If you were given a kit with hairbrush, comb (I mean seriously?) and nail clippers you will probably find a suitable file in there.

Nail clippers are a pain to use. They are fiddly at best and at worst, unless you have a magnifying glass to hand, it's all too easy to accidentally nip the skin under the baby's nail when using them. Babies don't exactly lie still when they are having personal treatments.

As a rule, waiting for baby to be milk-drunk is more likely to bring a better result when it comes to filing. When they are floppy and full, they are more co-operative. Gently file from the outer edge toward the middle top and repeat on the opposite side. Do each motion in one fluid movement rather than sawing.

Baby nails are quite soft so don't need much in the way of pressure. When the baby pulls back his hands and starts fussing, stop. It's polite. He is telling you he's had enough.

Make a mental note of which nails still need doing and try again a day later. By the time you have done all ten, the first two will need doing again anyway.

BATHTIME DRAMAS

Newborns don't like being naked for longer than a minute or two. In fact, most newborns hate being naked at all, and they will let you know this at every available opportunity.

They will cry when you undress them for nappy changes, and they will cry when you have to change wet or dirty clothes. They will cry when you undress them for baths and probably cry when Top & Tailing them too.

This is just their way of letting you know they feel vulnerable and don't like being over-handled.

You will learn that the best way to deal with this is just to get on with it as quickly and smoothly as you can, and also make the environment as warm and calm as you can.

If they are having a bit of a squawk whilst you wrestle with a nappy, try to resist continually picking them up for a cuddle. It simply prolongs the inevitable and has a tendency to make the whole tantrum escalate to biblical proportions.

Concentrate on getting the job done and then give him a long cuddle or a feed afterwards. Nappy changes are going to happen frequently, and this level of crying is yet another phase that they go through, but for now it is a bit of a shit fight.

DAD'S TIP

It can be quite nerve-wracking when the baby is shrieking as though you are boiling them in oil at each bath time, especially when the mother is elsewhere and might be wondering what on earth you are doing to your baby. Reassure her that all is well or invite her along to help if it is stressing you both out. Tag team.

All newborns really want to do when they are awake is feed. This is almost a "given" until they reach about 3/4 weeks old. If they are not fed fairly swiftly after waking, they will start to shout until you get your act together and present a meal! They have perfected a very loud inbuilt mechanism that makes sure that you meet their demands and it cannot be ignored.

As with every battle plan, better to stay one step ahead of the enemy so make sure you go through this list a day or so before you attempt bath time. I recommend that you tackle it a few times together before attempting to do it on your own.

- Prior to the bath, make sure the baby has had about half his feed — just to take the edge off the hunger. Look on it as a little bribe.

- If you are breastfeeding, get things ready beforehand.

- Make sure the bathroom is warm, closing all windows to reduce draughts. Lay out fresh clothes on the changing mat and have a clean nappy to hand.

In the bathroom, run the bath to 37°C. Some babies like it a little warmer, especially if their mum liked hot baths. Run the bath to give the bathroom a chance to warm up a little; check the water temperature using your bath thermometer; have two flannels or sponges (one for face and body, one for "bums and bits").

Put a folded towel (an old adult size towel is ideal) on the floor for extra padding/insulation. On top of this, spread out the baby's towel. If you have the space to have two changing stations in the house, then you can use the changing mat from one of them.

Wait for about 5-10 mins after the baby has fed, give his little bottom a clean and pop him into a fresh nappy, leaving that nappy on as you walk to the bathroom. If you take him through naked a) he may yell and b) he may wee or poo on you en route! Don't worry if he possets up a little of that last snack. This is not unusual and precisely why I say wait a few minutes after the feed.

Remove the clean nappy and then lower him gently into the bath. Keep slopping water over him so that he doesn't feel chilly or cover his torso with a wet flannel whilst you clean everything else. Wash around his ears, neck, face, arms, tummy and back with one sponge, and then with the other sponge do his armpits, legs and behind his knees, doing his bum & dangly bits or (girls) undercarriage last.

He may not be wild about baths when he is really tiny, but gradually he will grow to enjoy the whole experience. I find a fed baby is much more fun in the bath.

Only keep him in the water for about 5 minutes to start with and, once you have washed him, take him out if he is crying. Move him *slowly* through the air as you lift him out and onto his towel, so you don't chill him.

Wrap him up as quickly as you can and pat his head dry. Once babies are dry and feel warm, they tend to settle down. You can then pop him into his nappy, give him a little all over rub with some olive oil and carry him through to put his clean clothes on. After all this, he will be pretty exhausted and can then have the rest of his feed.

Products

Babies arrive into the world with a perfect little skin. It is advisable not to use *any* products on a baby's skin for the first few weeks. If they posset whilst lying down and their hair smells sicky, you can then use a little organic baby shampoo to help them smell nicer, but ideally, just use water.

Some babies will develop dry skin as their body grows bigger and they adapt to life outside the womb — especially those babies born in mid-winter when the heating is on and the air is dry.

CHAPTER 14

THEY SLEEP. THEY CRY.

"THE SYMPATHETIC NERVOUS SYSTEM IN A BABY IS DESIGNED TO
RELEASE ADRENALINE WHEN THEY BECOME OVERTIRED OR OVER
STIMULATED. IT IS A PRIMITIVE FLIGHT-OR-FIGHT RESPONSE".

New babies nap a lot and can only handle short periods of
stimulation. They need to feed frequently, returning to sleep
shortly after filling their tummies, so there is very little time in
which to "play" with your little one.

Their sleep patterns are, by nature, erratic and disorganised
and will remain this way until around 6 weeks old. It will therefore
be reassuring for you to know that their seemingly random timings are, in fact, to be expected.

Newborns, unable to cope with the chaos of our grown-up
timings outside the womb, tend to wake, eat and then return to
sleep fairly swiftly. They operate within in a window of time which
allows them space to eat and return to a sleepy state comparatively
quickly. This block of time is usually referred to as "The 90 Minute
Rule".

If you can keep an eye on this magic number, you may well find that your baby will find a perfect balance of sleep/eat/awake and you will avoid too many meltdowns.

The sympathetic nervous system in a baby is designed to release adrenaline when they become overtired or over stimulated. It is a primitive flight-or-fight response.

Therefore, it is essential for you to learn how to manage each Awake, Feed, Sleep cycle if you are to avoid many unhappy hours trying to soothe and calm your baby to sleep. If they are jittering because they are awash with adrenaline, you have little chance of being able to successfully settle them to sleep.

To prevent your newborn becoming overtired,
you must remember to focus on The 90 Minute Rule

Throughout the early weeks, babies can sleep for as much as 18 out of every 24 hours, but these little bouts of sleep are taken every couple of hours rather than in one giant block. Because parents are not used to periods of broken sleep, they tire much more quickly than the baby. When in this phase, it can feel as though your baby hardly sleeps at all.

Accept that for the first 6 weeks, your baby is quite likely to feed and then swiftly go back to sleep.

Occasionally he may be awake for up to 90 minutes, but more commonly you will find 70-75 minutes is more realistic.

THE WTF'S UP? GUIDE

Mums, Dads, Partners and Grandparents, please be aware that babies cry for many reasons. It is their only vocal means of communication when something is bothering them.

Learning to interpret your baby's "language" will start you on a much calmer road to understanding his needs and wants.

At times your baby will cry a great deal and sometimes they just cannot be comforted. This is no fault of yours and is a perfectly normal part of their development. Unfortunately, this knowledge does not make it any less stressful when experiencing it but should offer you some reassurance that it is not unusual.

Some people/books advise that if you keep him awake more in the day, you will get him to sleep longer at night. That may be the case when he is a few weeks older, but not so with newborns. More often than not, quite the opposite will happen. Your overwhelmed baby will become overtired and overstimulated. The outcome will be a miserable little mutineer who will be virtually impossible to calm down.

To a new parent, a crying baby always looks as though they are in acute pain. They pull up their legs, scrunch up their little face and squirm around, giving the impression that something is really hurting them. Confusingly, the body language can convey a multitude of mysterious messages, and I will do my best to help you unravel the code here.

You will probably find that the amount of crying will increase over the first 6-8 weeks until they reach their peak, then gradually become less and less. Peaks vary from baby to baby. Some peak around 3-4 weeks (if you are fortunate), others at 8 weeks. Some babies cry for long periods but not very often, while others often cry but not for long. Also, some babies spend more time fussing and less time crying inconsolably, while others cry a lot but not inconsolably. As frustrating as this is, it is a fact and simply makes it even harder for parents to come to terms with.

Generally, crying is divided up into three camps:

🧍 FUSSING

🧍 CRYING

🧍 INCONSOLABLE CRYING

Fussing: usually, the baby having a bit of a grump about something: a wet/dirty nappy, slight discomfort from intestinal wind, perhaps a residual burp or needing just a little bit more food.

Crying: a slightly more vocal way of trying to tell you something. Of course, if an adult were to cry in the same dramatic way as a baby, it would be perfectly reasonable to assume something had really upset them. But a baby cannot explain that they are feeling overtired, uncomfortable or just in need of a bit of peace and quiet, so they have a bit of a shout. They grimace and thrash their arms and legs about, perhaps looking as though they are in pain. But all these signs and signals can mean several things. As you get to know and understand your little one, you will soon begin to realise that they are usually (but not always) telling you something.

As a parent-detective, it is usually a simple process of elimination to arrive at the solution to the problem.

Crying could mean any of the following things:

- I'm too hot or a bit cold.
- I'm bored with this position.
- My nappy has leaked — can you change me?
- I have a little bit more wind to bring up; can you help me?
- I'm awake after my long nap and am hungry again.
- I'm ready for a nap and getting overtired now.
- I've been overhandled/passed around too many people and now I'm feeling overwhelmed.
- It's too bright/noisy in here, and I could do with some peace and quiet now.

Inconsolable Crying: A baby who cries inconsolably cannot be comforted no matter what tricks you pull out of the hat. The magic that worked yesterday and which suddenly resulted in a happy snoozer will today tip them into a whole new level of shoutiness.

For new parents, this can be scary, upsetting and often these bouts stop as quickly as they started leaving you battered, bewildered and feeling though you have just been shut in a coal bunker with a furious Honey Badger for two days. Suddenly out of nowhere, the baby falls into a deep and contented sleep, and you are left panting in the corner wondering what the hell it was all about.

You may never find out!

It is human nature to want an explanation. In episodes such as this, there will rarely be one, so the sooner you get to grips with that bit of news, the better you will feel about it when it happens. When it does, try to tag-team with your partner, a family member or anyone passing your front door who you may know and share the load.

It's hard to bond with a crying baby sometimes, and newborns do quite a lot of that to start with.

Manageable for the first couple of weeks, they may suddenly grow horns and a tail at about 2 weeks old, turning from angel to devil. They become demanding and fractious, often crying for hours yet not being soothed no matter what you do.

You might find it reassuring to learn that babies cry more in the first few weeks of life than at any other time; but it is understandable that this increase in crying will cause you, as new parents, a great deal of stress and anxiety during that time.

Desperate to find out what is "wrong" with your new baby, you may feel completely at a loss about how to comfort and calm him. Your Text Message Group may already be exploring medications, gripe water, infant antacids and checking in with the infamous Dr Google on a daily basis to find solutions.

This kind of crying is a very normal part of infant development, so while it is horrible when you are in the middle of it, this too will pass.

Infant crying peaks at around 4-6 weeks of age and most of that crying takes place in the late afternoon or evening. You may hear other mums talking of "The Witching Hours", or "Evening Fussing", and they are generally referring to this block of time in their days.

That is not to say that you should not seek support or advice and if you are worried, of course it is worth discussing your concerns with your Health Visitor, GP or Paediatrician.

THE EXCEPTIONS

There is an ever-increasing amount of evidence that tell us reflux is much more common in babies that first realised. What was labelled as Infant Colic a few years ago now seems to be more widely recognised as a *symptom* of one or more of the following:

- Reflux (also referred to as GORD)
- Silent Reflux
- Cow's Milk Protein Allergy
- Lactose Intolerance
- Dairy Intolerance
- Wheat Intolerance

- Reflux -

Reflux itself can also be a symptom of something else. I know! This all sounds confusing, but please bear in mind that advancements in the understanding of the gut and how it works is an ongoing study.

As the symptoms of reflux tend to appear after only a couple of weeks, they are frequently written off as being part of the normal, periodically cranky behaviour of a newborn. It is almost impossible to tell them apart without doing more detailed diagnostic tests. We don't have X-Ray vision, so sadly cannot be 100% sure without exploring a few options along the way.

Typically, a baby suffering with reflux will look and behave as though they are in severe pain, arching their backs and pulling up their knees whilst crying inconsolably. Confusingly, this behaviour is also common in newborns at other times (overtiredness and overstimulation for example), so muddying the waters further when trying to find the correct diagnosis.

Some will physically vomit up part or all of their feed, whilst others will bring up a little into their oesophagus and then swallow. The resulting burning sensation causes them to cry in pain and this is known as Silent Reflux.

In the case of reflux, the onset can be gradual, making it even harder to diagnose accurately. If a GP suspects reflux, you will normally be offered an antacid such as Infant Gaviscon. With limited appointment times available to investigate in depth, GPs tend to treat symptoms without really investigating the cause. As this level of antacid is quite weak, they often fail to make much difference, and because they contain a fair amount of sodium they will often lead to constipation, giving you yet another problem to deal with.

In the UK, where mild antacids don't diminish the symptoms, the next step seems to be referral to a GORD/Reflux specialist. In my experience, if they suspect reflux to be the cause of the discomfort, then a prescription medicine called Ranitidine is usually prescribed. This medication is also for heartburn and acid reflux, but just a bit stronger than Infant Gaviscon. Generally, it will take around 5-7 days before you see any improvement in your baby's behaviour.

If there is no improvement, then it is worth seeking expert advice in case your baby has any of the other allergies or intolerances listed above.

It is distressing for everyone when a baby is in pain or discomfort of any kind, but as I say, discovering where the problem lies can take time. Various options need to be explored and it may take several weeks before you have any answers.

If a Cow's Milk Protein allergy is suspected, then the advice is usually for a breastfeeding mother to cease consumption of all dairy products and, in the instance of formula fed babies, a different milk will be prescribed or recommended.

Reflux usually begins to improve after the three-month mark; allergies and intolerances will have to be monitored by your specialist.

Once the problem is identified, a simple change of diet or moving a baby onto goat's milk, specialist milk or medication can bring about dramatic changes in your baby's temperament. Please be patient with the people trying to help you. It is not a straightforward diagnosis and they will be trying their best.

Your little one's digestive system is still a work in progress, and it may be helpful if you can view the first 12 weeks of your baby's life as the 4th Trimester, not expecting too much from him. As he approaches 3 months of age, you should see these dramatic crying bouts diminish week by week.

Meanwhile, coping on a day to day basis can be exhausting and upsetting so it is important that you find someone to share the load from time to time. If your husband/partner has returned to work, chances are that you will be spending a great deal of time at home on your own. Try to connect with other mums in your area or call on friends and family to pop over to break up the day.

Being alone all day with a crying baby is exhausting and frustrating, so don't be afraid to pick up the phone and ask to go for a stroll with another mum. Even pluck up the courage to ring your neighbour's doorbell and pop in for a cup of tea and a natter. There is hardly a mum out there who has not had days just like this, so there is no shame in feeling you need company or a good cry yourself from time to time.

If there is a playground near where you live, chances are that there will be a bevy of mothers gathered there at various points of the day, desperate to let their children let off a bit of steam. Nothing starts a conversation here quicker than showing off a new baby and you will start to make connections before you know it.

You will be able to find a way to soothe your baby some of the time, but sometimes nothing works. This is normal, as are you and your baby.

- There is no QUICK FIX button -

If you are breastfeeding your baby, by the end of about Day 3 you may realise that it's not quite as easy as it looks in the movies. Babies often fuss at the breast, failing to make a good latch and you will be bombarded with lots of different advice/opinions from every angle.

Medical advancements in the past few years may be discovering that *colicky behaviour* is actually a sign of gastro oesophageal reflux (amongst other things).

Ten years ago we hadn't got the evidence on which to hang a definitive label, much less explain what it actually was; so it was included under the rather large umbrella heading as Colic.

This encompassed intestinal pain (farts on the move), reflux, burping, evening fussiness, prolonged bouts of crying, knees being pulled up and general crankiness. Not very helpful really.

The fact that it was always referred to as Three Month Colic by not only my mother's generation, but many GPs I've met over the years, meant that many babies were not diagnosed with reflux caused by allergies until well into their 3rd or 4th month of life. A miserable situation for any new mother.

Over the past 24 years, I have been called in to help out with babies supposedly suffering from "colic" more times than I can count. Despite conflicting diagnoses from GPs or Health Visitors, it was reassuring that a large percentage of those babies' symptoms improved once better feeding patterns were implemented.

Of those who continued to be unsettled despite having nicely spaced feeds and plenty of sleep in between, there was often an underlying cause such as lactose intolerance, cow's milk protein allergy or silent reflux.

Babies have a very immature digestive system. It is hardly surprising that when they are born it takes a while for that system to adjust to regular feed-awake-sleep patterns as well as the stimulation of everyday life. The muscles which regulate the transportation of the stomach contents through the digestive tract are not fully developed and, as with all their other muscles, will become so given time.

In this age of instant gratification, there is no Quick Fix button. So, while I have worked with many babies who went on to be diagnosed with allergies, reflux or intolerances — it is often worth checking to see that you are not fracturing their sleep-feed-awake cycle too badly before you assume a medical condition.

It is a growing problem in this technological age. Everyone becomes an expert at the click of a button. Unfortunately, Cyberchondria, as it is now called, tends to fuel anxiety rather than alleviate it. Scan-reading a mummy forum on some dubious source or scrolling through baby-related web pages online in a sleep-deprived haze at 3am is not conducive to reliable research.

Another source of angst amongst new mothers is the ubiquitous Text Messaging Groups. Although a wonderful method for keeping contact with your antenatal groups, they can prove to be the epitome of The Blind Leading the Blind. First time mums begin texting their concerns and questions to each other week on week, and before you know it, everyone becomes an expert, and this is the result:

- Someone in the group has popped in a few choice phrases into an on-line search and then read that a baby may have "colic" or "reflux" on a forum.

- They are given several promised cure-all medicines to try. They have success with one product.

- They post this triumph in the group.

- They group go dashing off to the chemist or GP to medicine-match whatever their Text Group buddy has been given, believing their baby's problem is the same.

👶 Their baby continues to be unsettled, so they feel frustrated.

👶 They go back to the GP demanding a second opinion or buy another cure-all.

… and so on.

Again, my advice is to use group chats to keep in touch, stay sane, be supportive and arrange meetups. When it comes anything medical, try to avoid passing on what may well be incorrect information and leave that to the experts.

If your baby seems to be constantly unsettled, constantly in pain during or after feeds or begins to battle with feeds, then it may be worth speaking to your GP about the possibility of an allergy or intolerance. Sometimes it as simple as removing dairy or wheat from the mother's diet (which obviously only applies to breast fed babies); otherwise it could be an intolerance to a certain make of formula

To help keep your baby calm and rested, focus on establishing good sleep patterns. Give your baby a chance to sleep, digest and grow. Offer him stimulation at a level relative to his age/capability in the daytime and give regular feeds that are structured not fractured, distracted or foreshortened. Remember, try to manage your own expectations of your little person — they can't cope with much for a few weeks. Your smiling face and interaction will be called upon soon enough.

What you expect vs. what you're going to get

One of my pet hates in the world of written advice to parents is the inappropriate use of the word "should". This implies that if a baby fails to do whatever the author declares it "should" be doing, the parent has in some way failed to meet some imagined standard.

Examples of this are:

- By 16 weeks old your baby **should** sleep through the night.
- An 8-week-old baby **should** have 7oz of formula per feed.
- By 12 weeks old your baby **should** be able to roll over.

You might find that if you mentally substitute the word *should* for *may*, you view things a little differently.

Your baby may roll over as early as 12 weeks old. However, as all babies develop at different rates, this might not happen until he is a few months older.

In this example, had I put "Your baby should roll over at 12 weeks old", you would be fretting about their physical development if yours is still lying firmly on his back at 16 weeks with that "Bring me a beer, bitch" look on his face.

I worked with twins a few years ago — both boys. One rolled at 8 months. I don't think he planned it. To say that he didn't like it would be an understatement. For one split second, he looked at me as though someone had just shouted BUMHOLE in front of the Pope! He then burst into tears and took about half an hour to recover.

He didn't try rolling again for another two months.

His brother turned over the following week, and it was as

if someone had given him free airline travel for a month — he was OFF! Clocking up serious mileage, frequently to be found repetitively doinking his head against a skirting board like some demented clockwork toy. Rescued with a deft and timely assisted spin through 180°, he was then able to launch himself off towards the opposite wall.

He was happy for hours! Strictly Come Rolling had arrived.

Different strokes for different folks. They both got there in their own sweet time and now, aged 6, they dance like no-one is watching. So, who are we to say they *should* do anything?

Of course, on a serious note: if your baby does not meet certain developmental milestones there may be an underlying cause, but regular check-ups with your doctor/baby clinic will go a long way towards alleviating any unnecessary fretting.

For the first few months, babies need to nap frequently. Easing your baby into a gentle and flexible daily pattern will help you feel a little less out of control and better able to plan your days. You'll notice I don't use the words "Timetable" or "Schedule". You have a baby, not a bus.

In this book, I've tried to use the word routine or pattern. This is to make the edges of any curfew a little blurrier and looser.

No hard and fast times, no scheduled activity, no strict rules.

Earlier in this section I mentioned viewing the first 12 weeks as the 4th Trimester. It's possible you will hear this phrase more frequently now, so worth keeping in mind. If more parents did so, they may find these early weeks less stressful.

By setting expectations too high in the early weeks, believing a baby to be far more capable or advanced than they actually are, many parents struggle. They feel frustrated that their baby won't adhere to the guidelines laid out in the plethora of baby books. Finding that the baby behaves beautifully one day and like a child possessed the next leads to clutching at straws and desperately trying to regain control and structure.

Elation and relief one day will be swiftly followed the next by crushing overwhelm and exhaustion. This is your new normal. Tiredness is normal, frustration normal, tears and tantrums (yours, as well as the baby's) … yes, all normal. But one thing I can assure you is that it will, and it does, evolve.

It doesn't get better. It doesn't get worse. It gets different.

You didn't have any expectations of him when he was still curled up inside you, so you must cut him some slack now. Gently ease him through the first three months by adopting healthy habits, offering love and comfort and slowly build your baby a secure, safe and flexible family routine over several weeks.

Babies who have had a rather rude arrival into the world (by way of forceps delivery or Ventouse/vacuum method), have usually done so after a problematic birth. They may well have been "stuck" for some time, with all manner of clamping and pushing going on around their tiny frames. Understandably, these babies can be quite traumatised after such an event.

Conversely, some babies arrive in the world with a bang, crying often and loudly which, to a first-time parent, can be frazzling, to say the least. Rest assured; it is usually not because you are doing anything "wrong". But there may be an underlying issue, particularly if they have had forceps or Ventouse delivery. This is where osteopathy may help.

Osteopathy was covered in more detail back in Chapter 8. If this gentle treatment is something you feel may be helpful, it is ideal to get your baby seen sooner rather than later. Seek out a cranial osteopath who specialises in treating babies, often referred to as a paediatric osteopath.

Tensions in their head, neck, jaw, hips or diaphragm may well affect other areas such as feeding positioning at the breast, reflux, ability to feed well on a bottle, passing wind or pooing without discomfort.

In the postnatal fog that will be the first 3 months, you may well feel that you are stuck in a very repetitive and exhausting time-freeze. Each day blurring into the next, for weeks on end. Take heart — this will change as you adapt to your new role as a mother.

For now, focus on making sure that your new baby is fed well approximately every 2-3.5 hours to start with, easing him gently towards 3.5-4 hours over a few weeks. Sometimes your baby may regularly manage 3-4 hours between feeds, and if that is at night then that is a bonus. Everyone gets a bit more sleep.

Concentrate on seizing the moment. This is the time when your baby will learn habits. You have a completely empty vessel. Whatever habits you work on now will help build a baby who will nap well and self-settle. Flexible routines and more structured days will follow once the baby is up and running.

Also, try to keep telling yourself that things happen in chunks. The first two weeks is a helluva chunk and a hugely steep learning curve for all first-time parents. Breastfeeding will settle down, shouty nappy changes will settle down, poo frequency will settle down and the crying (which increases before it decreases) will settle down.

You will be living in phases of around 2-3 weeks and each time you get to the end of one phase, take time to look over your shoulder and see how far you have come.

For the first week or two, you may find that your baby is a little feeding/sleeping machine. This is frequently the case with C-section babies. They have not had the birth experience so, initially, take time to realise they are actually born.

One minute they are snuggled up in the womb, the next they are being pulled out through the sunroof. It's not surprising that they curl into a little sleepy ball and wait until they feel ready before starting to express themselves more forcefully.

Parents are often lulled into a false sense of security, believing they have the best behaved and easiest baby that was ever born. Try not to label them too quickly. They change at a rate of knots and the baby you have in Week One may be a totally different experience by the end of Week Two.

You may feel a little disappointed if you were expecting a gurgling, grinning little person, gazing lovingly at you as you change nappies and bathe them. Babies are just not capable of that level of interaction at this age. They develop at different rates and whilst there are guideline markers along the way, every baby ticks boxes in their own time.

I have known a baby smile properly at only three weeks old, yet many experts say they only start at around six weeks. I've seen babies who could roll over repeatedly at eight weeks, yet we are told that rolling only starts at around 3-4 months. We are back to the "should" vs the "may" argument again. I'd suggest hitting a batting average and be happy with that.

Remember, babies cry and sometimes nothing can be done that seems to console them.

All babies fuss at some point in their day and for a variety of reasons. It is not always something you need to "fix" or stop. Often it is not that your baby is unhappy, in pain or hungry, but just having a bit of a shout and expressing himself the way babies always have.

I hope that by reading this book, you will be better able to decipher what they need from you and understand the differences between an "I need ...." from an "I want..." when it comes to crying.

THE SLEEP WINDOW

Most newborns can only handle a maximum of 90 minutes of Happy Awake time before they need to go back to sleep again. Happy Awake, as the name implies, is the time when they are not fussing or shouting about something.

Generally speaking, if being fed or otherwise entertained, they are Happy Awake. After Happy Awake they move to Thrashy, then to Fussy and from Fussy to Shouty.

This last stage is referred to as Missing Your Sleep Window (if Mum does it) or Buggering It Up (if Dad does it)!

Ideally, we want to avoid you getting to Shouty if you have a hope of getting him down without all the dramatics

By recognising how long your baby can cope with being awake before moving from Happy to Fussy, you will master the art of being One Step Ahead.

Of course, having worked with armies of babies over the past 24 years, I have a distinct advantage. I spent years with the little stinkers before I rumbled that they all have similar body language. It's hardly surprising when you think about it. In the same way that adult humans display signs of stress, exhaustion, tiredness, pleasure or irritation — so do babies.

Once I'd experienced that lightbulb moment, I began to take notes with each new baby job. I observed that they all have very similar ways of displaying with their faces, bodies and sounds, giving you clues to communicate their various requirements.

I moved from family to family, building up my experience, watching and learning how these little people speak to us. It was a revelation. There were no Baby Bibles back then. I have been able to build up my knowledge and expertise through experience and am now aiming to pass some tips on to you.

HANDS UP ANYONE WHO WANTS GOOD SLEEP HABITS

A newborn has no guile, but babies quickly learn habits that are the result of a parent taking the line of least resistance. Of course, a baby would probably fall asleep more rapidly if allowed to doze off draped over a shoulder or in a lap. But once the baby is asleep, the weary parent tries to decant the sleeping baby into a cot, only to find that the moment they are put down, they wake up and begin crying. Exasperating.

When it comes to helping babies learn how to settle to sleep, surely it makes more sense to implement habits that are sustainable in the longer term? I'm not saying that you should not have that magical time of having your gently breathing baby fall asleep on your shoulder or curled up in your lap — but just making you aware of the habits you may inadvertently be creating if you do it *every* time.

You know, that tiny little Bumble-Bee-Bum in a white onesie, all cute and sleep-warm next to your cheek? Well, he bangs out some serious transformational moves in the next stages, growing in and out of five sizes of baby-grows like the Incredible Hulk and BLAM!

Before you can say "Nappy Rash", there on your shoulder lies a snoring 6kg, 12-week old giving you a dead arm and backache because you are too terrified to even *think* about moving for two hours in case he wakes up.

Try to start as you mean to go on and keep asking yourself "Do I still want to be doing this in a year?" If the answer is no, then you have a good chance of getting off on the right foot by adopting the system that will work in the longer term.

One wise Grandmother said to me that she had a similar quote which she had passed on to her daughter: "Whatever it is you are doing to get him to sleep, you must be prepared to do it two thousand times".

I think that just about sums it up.

Creating bad sleep habits is relatively easy compared to the extra work and perseverance required for good sleep habits.

As you crash through month one at home as a family, you will be witnessing your baby getting to grips with life in the world of noise, nappy changes and feeds. Along with this, you have a baby who almost inevitably will have grumbly guts, trapped burps, and a seemingly insatiable appetite.

If you are to have any hope of getting some structure to your days, it is imperative to begin at basement level as you build your baby's sleep habits. I am not suggesting a strict 4-hourly feeding schedule or any kind of timetable. I am talking about a loose, flexible routine which you will hone, adapt and become familiar with over the first 6-8 weeks.

This way day by day, week by week, you will learn to deal with the knockbacks, the frustration and the chaos that this new mini mutineer will inflict upon your planned day.

TEACHING A BABY TO SETTLE TO SLEEP

As with most things baby related, there are many opinions about the "correct" way of helping babies off to the Land of Nod.

The opposing views can become heated and on occasion, quite judgmental. However, they are all just opinions and you can form your own.

Some of my peers did not follow any form of routine, and I have visited many clients with babies aged 4-6 months who were desperate to teach them to settle to sleep on their own. I've also taken many bookings with parents expecting their second baby who, with the benefit of sleep deprived hindsight, accept that the methods they employed first time round simply won't work when you have two to deal with. They all regretted not starting off with better foundations. As a result, it is my belief that implementing healthy sleep habits as early as possible will stand you in good stead in the long run.

I am not talking militant routines, delaying feeding or leaving young babies to cry for hours without responding. I'm talking about the introduction of sleep associations and settling patterns gradually over a few weeks, creating habits that can be carried forward rather than having to suffer the misery of sleep training or living with fractured nights and chaotic days for months to come. And yes, it can be months, and sometimes, years!

It is heaven to allow your baby to stay nestled on your shoulder after a lovely, snuggly feed. But it is worth bearing in mind that in the longer term this is not a sustainable way of putting the baby to sleep. It is surprising how quickly a teeny, tiny little 3.5kg baby turns into a small hippopotamus. When that hippopotamus is then parked permanently on your shoulder and unable to settle to sleep in their own bed simply because they have never learned how, life may become exceptionally trying.

"Oh, but," I hear you bleat, "can't we just do that for a *little* while and then move them to their bed in a few weeks?" Sure, you can. Or rather, you can try.

Over the *few weeks* you have employed the shoulder sleeping position, you will have successfully taught your baby to sleep a) on a nice warm human and b) on their fronts. We all know that front-sleeping for very young babies is considered a no-no, and of the many hundreds of recommendations that have been bandied around over the past few years, the "Back to Sleep" campaign has resulted in a massive decline in SIDS. Irrefutable, undeniable fact.

If you teach a baby that your shoulder is the place to sleep, then that is where they will happily remain. Yet when the time comes that you decide you cannot really do this after each and every feed, and now you want to put the baby on their back in their cot, you will almost certainly find that the baby will, figuratively speaking, stand with their little hands planted on their hips and muster a small rebellion. And rightly so! This is not how or where he was taught to sleep, and this new Cot Rule will not be passed at Baby Parliament without a great deal of huffing and puffing... but it will be passed.

Thus, this serves to re-enforce the fact that you can make a different habit stick by repetition. It is how the brain learns.

I think I can safely say that most people sleep with a pillow under their heads in this country. If someone were to sneak into my room one day and remove not only my pillows but those in the shops for miles around, what would happen?

And let's not get silly. Suggesting that I order some from Amazon Prime or get some down from the loft is not clever, and it's not funny. Well, actually it is a bit funny, but work with me and try to appreciate the analogy I am trying to create.

If I did not have a pillow but usually slept with one, there is going to be one outcome over the next few nights. Either I will stay awake for several days straight, or, after a bit of huffing and puffing and readjustment, I will learn to sleep without a pillow.

Your babies can learn to settle to sleep under their own steam, without your needing to give them any assistance at all, if you put in the groundwork at the very beginning. Babies learn by repetition, and by starting out with sustainable sleep habits you will save yourselves a lot of heartache further down the line.

I know that when I am doing a gym session, unless my trainer is physically standing over me, I notice that my cheat of a body will always seek out a less strenuous way of performing various exercises. It is human nature for us to choose an easier path, the path of less resistance.

Therefore, if parents are not prepared to put in the groundwork to establish a stable foundation on which to build good habits, then the outcome will be wholly predictable, and they will have a baby that never learns to fall asleep unaided.

When I first speak to a potential client, and they ask what "methods" I use, they often assume I have one recipe, one set of inflexible instructions which I apply to each and every baby with whom I work.

This is not so. I spend time developing a structure with both the baby and the parents — much as one might build a house — and I would encourage you to do the same. Start with the foundations, introducing little healthy habits, correcting and tweaking things that don't quite work, until the base structure is sound. Once you have done that, you then hang out there for a while before moving on up the ladder and begin developing the next level. Does that make sense?

Babies arrive into this world with two fears: falling (being dropped) and sudden loud noises.

When a baby is adequately fed, has shown they are tired and are then put down to sleep in their cot, the transition from drowsy to asleep involves a period where they feel as though they are falling.

Think about it. When you lie down to go to sleep, do you simply close your eyes and that is it? You are asleep. Or do you slowly drift from drowsy, to light dreams and then gradually into a deep sleep? When I ask my clients, the usual response is the latter.

During the drowsy stage of the process, it is common to feel as though you are falling. As though you are about to plummet from a great height; we snap ourselves awake with a sharp intake of breath, only to instantly realise that we were simply "falling asleep".

Bingo! Falling. Falling Asleep.

Is it any wonder that a tiny baby reacts to the sensation by jumping, thinking that they are falling? Does it not then make equal sense that frequently offering your baby reassurance at this stage will help them to become accustomed to the sensation and go with it?

They will gradually learn that they are safe and secure in their little bed, not falling from a great height. In a short time, they will only fuss and fidget, wriggle and grizzle a little before allowing themselves to drift gently off to sleep, but only if you respect what they are trying to do and give them space and time they need to experiment.

It is quite possible that by using props to coax your baby to sleep, (or indeed become the prop yourself), your baby will become dependent on that prop each and every time he needs to go to sleep.

Many couples resort to walking for hours to get the baby to sleep or taking them everywhere in a sling against their chest. However, sleeping like this just does not compare to the deep and restorative sleeps a young baby has in their own bed. Chatter, traffic noise, regular bumps and bangs in a buggy will disrupt the brain patterns as the baby snoozes, even when they appear to be fast asleep and over time, this will result in your baby's ability to sleep deeply becoming more and more erratic.

I'm not suggesting that you can never go for walks like this, but in the early weeks it is so important to establish a) a good nap pattern on a daily basis and b) to do all you can to enable your baby to have a quiet sleep in their own bed. Invest heavily over the first three months by allowing your little one to sleep well in their own bed as much as possible.

If you enjoy nursing your baby to sleep on the breast or holding them on your shoulder for hours during the day, maybe co-sleeping at night, or perhaps pounding the streets with the baby in the buggy to keep them asleep, that is your right and your privilege. But for those who would like to have more routine, more predictability and the certainty that when they are put down in their cots, they will settle themselves down, then read on.

Teaching a baby to settle on their own takes time, patience and repetition. The earlier you start, the easier it will be. When you arrive home with your baby, you have a clean canvas, a baby who has not yet learned anything, so why not try to help them to learn something that, in the long run, will be sustainable for both them and for you?

Sleep Associations can be simple things such as swaddling them as they start to tire, perhaps saying Goodnight to a teddy bear or closing the curtains as you sing a little song before putting them in their cot. It is all about the repetition; one action always precedes another.

With older babies, you give them a story, kiss and a cuddle before settling them down. The sleep association may have morphed from a simple swaddle to a cuddly toy. More often than not, this will be some rather manky and pungent bit of much-loved muslin they have sucked and chewed since they were 4 months old.

The familiarity of repetition to a baby is beyond measure. I have seen some of my babies positively wilt with relief when they are back in their own home after a few days in unfamiliar surroundings. They love being back in their room, with their familiar routines.

DUMMIES

Otherwise known by our friends over the pond as Pacifiers.

As you romp through these pages, you will begin to get the message that I am a huge fan of teaching babies good sleep habits. These habits should be the very foundations of what you want your kids to be doing within just a few months. This process takes time, dedication and patience.

When spending time with new parents, I am often asked about the use of dummies. Now, having worked in London for many years I've met a very diverse group of mums and amongst their number, an orthodontist and a dentist. On each occasion, it has been the perfect moment for me to have a chat about the perceived evils of dummies and their effect upon a baby's teeth.

Given that we are covering the first three months of life in this book, I sincerely hope that your baby hasn't yet got teeth and will assume that they will not put in an appearance until your baby reaches 4-6 months of age before they do.

The orthodontist confidently informed me that using a dummy will have no ill effect on a baby's teeth, even if the baby continues to use the dummy after the milk teeth have started to come in. If it is solely used for soothing a baby to sleep, it will be fine. If they are still walking around with it as a permanent face fixture when they are three? Meh! Doesn't rock my world, but it's your child and therefore your call.

I don't use dummies for an entirely different reason. They are a habit, and they will turn full circle from feeling like a *solution* to a problem to a problem that needs to be solved.

I am a very vocal promoter of cementing sustainable habits. Ones that don't require correcting or re-training months, years down the line. The sobbing and possibly highly volatile reaction that "The Dummy Fairy needs your dummy for other babies in the world" conversation elicits, but with a three-year-old who cannot speak coherently (without having first to remove the plastic plug from his mouth) is not something I wish for you.

Here's what often happens on the Dummy Timeline:

It's Week 2: you are both staggering around in a state of sunken-eyed sleep deprivation. Your baby has been angelic all day. At night babies often seem to shapeshift, becoming a whole different person. With their seemingly bat-like precision radar, your night-baby appears to be able to detect the exact second the fork pierces the first slice of warm food you've managed to get onto a plate all day.

That is the moment the baby monitor springs into life, and you hear, "Eh… eh … eh", which heralds the start of the Shouty Olympics.

Noooooo! This cannot be happeninnnng!

Not twenty minutes earlier he'd gone down. Pink and soft after his relaxing bath and having spent a good hour welded to the sofa to make sure that things were kept, as all baby books advise, calm and quiet, you'd satiated him with all his little tummy could hold.

You then carried his flollopy body to the nursery. You gently wrapped him up in his swaddle before delicately laying him down in his cot.

Chubby-cheeked and panting as though he'd just devoured the calorific equivalent of a small artic seal, it seemed unthinkable that he could possibly want for more. You'd turned the lights off and backed nervously out of the door, avoiding every one of the creaky floorboards (by now demarcated with duct tape covered with luminous paint) and tiptoed downstairs, silently air punching on every step.

Peachy!

A thoughtful gift of home-made meals winked at you from the fridge earlier, and you'd had the foresight to put it in the oven in advance.

A bottle of chilled Chablis was leaning up against a pint of milk in the fridge door like a Soho hooker, and in your sleep deprived state you could swear it beckoned and winked at you. Another air punch. You'd both collapsed in a heap feeling like a great team.

Then, right on cue: Eh Eh EH! You whimper and slump forwards; your shoulders sag. Forks clatter onto the plates. Desperate, hollow-eyed looks are exchanged as you both sigh and carry the food back to the kitchen.

The opening ceremony for the Shouty Olympics has begun, and you realise that you'll probably have toast for supper at midnight, and you watch as the wine saunters back into the darkness of the fridge without a backward glance.

It is entirely understandable that after several nights of this, many parents will resort to the use of a dummy. It's a quick fix to an exhausting problem.

While babies are very young, most of them can easily suck a dummy when it is introduced. For the first several weeks of their life, babies have a strong suck reflex, so it's effortless for them to keep the dummy in their mouths as they drift off to sleep. But the downside comes when it either falls or is pushed out.

By introducing a dummy at this stage, a habit is quickly formed, and in a short time, the baby will expect it to be present to fall asleep.

Now, I'm not saying that you should not use one to soothe, or that they don't have their moments. I am merely pointing out that you may well create a sleep prop. That prop will come back to bite you on the bum in a few weeks or months if you are not mindful about how you employ it.

Initially the baby will probably tongue-thrust the dummy out of his mouth in his sleep. When a little older, he will pull it out with his hands. Either way, your presence will be required to put it back in again.

Babies, like adults, sleep in cycles. During each of these cycles, we fall into a deep sleep and then come into a lighter phase before returning to deep sleep again.

When babies are very young, and before they have mastered falling asleep under their own steam, they hit the first lighter phase of sleep where they may awaken briefly. Ideally, you want to gently teach them how to join these two chapters of sleep together without any intervention needed from you.

If you use a dummy to put your baby to sleep, he will find it very hard to enter this light phase and return to sleep without your having to employ the trick you used to put him to sleep in the first place. Hence, guess who has to trundle back and forth to the cot to keep putting it back in? Yep — you do!

Now, forgive me pointing out the bleedin' obvious here, but when you introduced the dummy in the first place, wasn't the idea to facilitate more chill out time or get some sleep yourselves?

Hmmm? Thought so. But if I have got this right, you are now having to go back in every 20-40 minutes to re-insert the dummy to keep the baby asleep, right? This way lies madness.

Wouldn't it be better to invest the time at the start, to help your baby learn how to not only drift off to sleep in the first instance but to join the two or three sleep cycles together until he is ready to feed again?

Perhaps keep the dummy for those occasions when you have tried everything else and everyone just needs to sleep. If you only use it now and then, it will not become a habit. Aim to stop using it at all after your baby passes the 6 Week mark.

All too often, I have been to visit parents who, when baby awakens after one sleep cycle, rush in at the first squeak and pick them up. The baby didn't need anything; he was just stirring and having a little grizzle. He was still tired, a bit groggy and not yet hungry. Yet having picked him up you will almost certainly fully rouse him.

There, blinking and cross in your arms, you have one bad situation. A baby who is not well rested and is not yet hungry.

A weapon of mass destruction in a nappy. Good luck with that!

FIZZY DAYS!

Imagine you are in a room in a house with a big window. Hanging from the curtain rail there are 15 net curtains, limiting your view to the fields outside to little more than a blur of light and shade. That is pretty much what visual life is like for a newborn; unable to see much beyond his mother's face in any degree of focus. Rather like wearing a really bad pair of glasses.

Each time your baby goes through a growth phase, one or two of those net curtains is pulled to the side. The outside world is bought into sharper focus. It's rather like being given a new pair of glasses a year after you suspected you really needed an upgrade.

To a baby, this process can be a little unsettling. No sooner have they learned to feel comfortable in their blurry little world than BLAM! ... things change. Understandably, this can make them feel wobbly for a few days as they settle into their newfound skill set.

Coupled with the new glasses, all kinds of changes are going on inside that little head. Sections of the brain that govern cognition, movement, language, and emotional skills are developing, and that results in all kinds of ups and downs with behaviour. I call these times "Fizzy Days".

During Fizzy Days, you may find your baby clings to you when you are holding them; little fists scrunched closed around a fold in your sleeve, like a koala bear. The world can seem like a big and scary place as these changes come about.

Be patient with them when they are like this — and let them get used to their "new spectacles". Wait for the Fizzy Feelings to fade and allow them time to become familiar with their new development.

It's quite helpful to note anticipated Growth Spurt dates on your kitchen calendar, highlighting them with a yellow or bright red marker pen. That way, when he throws you a Fizzy Day or two, you can refer to the calendar just for reassurance that this is normal and, as with most phases, will pass in time.

Many view growth spurts as a period where the baby simply feeds more often and gains more weight quite rapidly in that time. However, there is more going on behind the scenes than that.

While the baby may indeed grow chubbier as a result of the increased intake of food, this feeding frenzy will be helping to build their "circuit board", their brain. Both before and after each growth spurt, you may notice subtle changes in your baby's behaviour.

At around this time babies can often feel a little out of sorts. They may be clingy, needing comfort and cuddles while they get used to sensations occurring in their little bodies and heads.

They may be grumpier and crankier than usual and as a result, they may cry more for a few days. Give them time to adapt to those changes and offer reassurance as they go through them. Once they feel more at ease with this new perception of their world you can back off and leave them to it

Be mindful of the fact that these phases seldom last long. You simply have to roll with the punches and then re-calibrate to put yourself back on track.

UNDERSTANDING HOW BABIES SLEEP

Whilst your baby has been developing in the womb, they have had everything delivered directly to their door with the reliability of an Ocado order. Mum's body takes care of all their needs: climate control (temperature), oxygen, food and even sewage management. Fantastic things, these mums.

In the womb a baby does actually have a sleep/awake cycle, and this becomes more noticeable during the final weeks of pregnancy as he seemingly snoozes quietly at some points of the day, only to spring into action by bopping around and kicking at others.

This is known as the Ultradian Rhythm and, after the baby is born, he will gradually shift across to our own more Circadian Rhythms. This shift will begin at around 6 weeks of age when a baby's system begins to produce melatonin. Melatonin is a hormone and it is this that regulates the body's sleep/awake cycles.

For those of you reading this who were not entirely sure whether Circadian Rhythm is a biological fact or just a new band from the X-Factor, I will give you a dictionary definition because I am not a doctor and I don't want you thinking I made it all up.

- Ultradian rhythm -

Ultradian rhythm is a biological rhythm that occurs with a frequency of less than 24 hours. Sleep is composed of several repetitive cycles of about 90 minutes in length. The sleep cycle is composed of two types of sleep: REM (Rapid Eye Movement) and non-REM sleep.

- Circadian rhythms -

Circadian rhythms are physical, mental, and behavioural changes that follow a daily cycle. They respond primarily to light and darkness in an organism's environment.

Sleeping at night and being awake during the day is an example of a light-related circadian rhythm. Circadian rhythms are found in most living things, including animals, plants and many tiny microbes.

Once your baby bounds into the world, their body has to learn to take over and go it alone. Hundreds of experiences are thrown at them during the first few days: Sounds, sights and smells rain down on them from all angles.

Their nervous system is bombarded by nappy changes, applications of potions and lotions, cuddles and kisses from perfume drenched, loud and doting relatives, all eager to say hello. It is hardly surprising that they can become irritable and shouty pretty early on.

As your baby's body begins to take charge of its own bio-rhythms, they leap in and out of different states.

The ebb and flow of your previously predictable lives has been thrown into turmoil for a while. Accept that, where previously you could bimble along to your own rhythm, you are now answering to the beat of a different drum. Your baby's vastly different beat.

Where adults sleep in cycles of 90 minutes, a baby's is 45 minutes. Where adults tend to eat approximately every 6-7 hours, babies need to fill up anywhere from 2-4 hourly. Where we adults drop off the loo-luggage once a day, babies are the equivalent of a luggage carousel at Heathrow Airport in August. A relentless turnover, several times a day to start with.

Life is about to change, my friend!

Over the coming weeks it is important for you to set aside some time each day just observing. Not playing with, not entertaining, not cuddling or chatting … just observing.

Try to choose a time immediately after a feed and pop him down on a rug or playmat and just watch. After a few weeks, babies love interaction and face to face contact, but right now they find it very tiring, so allow them time to simply BE!

Let them lie on a soft mat, staring at nothing in particular, and you may notice that although they are fairly still, their eyes are flicking around the room. They can't see much at all, but they will be processing all the sights, contrasts of light, sounds and sensations. Their body and limbs may move a little here and there, but they show no signs of distress.

When you do engage in play, notice when your baby begins to look away from you, or tries to disengage from some object that you are waving in their face. Keep an eye on them to see when they start to yawn, fuss or begin to get more agitated. These are all little clues that you, as a new parent, must learn to pick up if you are to anticipate your baby's needs. It is a lovely little language and, if you tune into it early on, it saves many miserable hours jiggling a shouty baby whose clues you missed.

There are dozens of baby books out there and hidden amongst their pages you will find some little nugget, an observation or tip which will be helpful. However, when I am coaching my clients, I emphasise that you must also simply spend time *observing* your babies and realise that everything is very new to them.

In my pre-baby-coaching life, I was a S.C.U.B.A. diving instructor and underwater photographer. (Seriously — if you can imagine trying to sneak up on a school of fish for a perfect shot, you will understand the meaning of extreme patience: skills that have served me well for the past 24 years).

"Fish? Diving? What? Where the hell is she going with this?" I hear you ask.

When I first arrived, by boat, on the Maldivian island of Vilamendhoo I was bewitched. Seas twinkling with the stars of a thousand aquamarines, no discernible horizon to divide it from the cloudless sky. Tropical fish of every shape and size darting around meters below me and shrubs covered with flowers, smothered with startlingly bright flowers. It was a sensory overload and

I walked to my little hut in complete disbelief. There was no need for a welcoming chorus from flower bedecked, grass skirted hula-hula girls on the end of the jetty to enhance the experience. The island was enough.

Your home is the Maldives to your new baby. An experience like no other he has had in his life — all 48 hours of it! There is no need to whip out the playmat, the musical mobile or Aunty Gwen's 8th generation teddy bear just yet. Your sitting room is Vilamend-hoo — no hula-hula girls required, thank you kindly. Now, bring me my welcome drinks.

In the early weeks, babies tire rapidly. As a result, it becomes pretty important to capitalise on the awake times and ensure your baby has a lovely big feed. Once a newborn is satiated, they need to return to a sleep state quickly. The time for hula-hula girls and such things is a little way off yet.

Your baby needs time to start processing his new world and all the sensations he has to encounter on a minute by minute basis.

It might help to have this little checklist to start with. Observe your baby immediately after the feed and you will begin to mentally catalogue these physical clues:

- Looking away from toys or your face
- His body becoming still and calm for brief moments
- A short shout out or bleat
- Gazing into the middle distance
- Slow blink rate
- The first yawn

When these signs are ignored or overlooked he will become

twitchy, agitated or fretful and will then certainly begin telling you that he has had enough. You must respect this body language and act on it, removing him from that situation by taking him to somewhere less stimulating — ideally his nursery cot or to his crib in your bedroom.

Once swaddled and put down, he may well lie awake for up to 20 minutes, staring at the walls but calm and quiet. This is called the Quiet Awake state.

SLEEP STATES

- Deep sleep -

Your baby will be breathing regularly, sometimes almost imperceptibly (just to keep you on the edge!) and will be very still.

- Light sleep -

This state is also known as REM (Rapid Eye Movement) sleep or, in dog language, "Chasing Bunnies" sleep. His breathing will be more irregular, perhaps panting a little as his face twitches, his eyes flicker open and closed again and he may jump at little noises going on around him. Creaking floorboards, door handles which click when turned or blind pulls ticking against a window frame may cause him to startle. It is during this phase that babies may cry as they learn to drift off. Try to give them a bit of space and allow them time to work it out. If they need a little help in the early weeks, then return to soothe them before popping them down to try again.

- Drowsy -

Drowsy is that in-between time either as they drift off to sleep or as they are coming out of a long sleep.

- Quiet alert -

Quiet alert is two bright little eyes blinking back up at you from the cot, but they are still and calm. When they are like this, leave them be. They are in a form of meditative state, processing the smallest of sensations such as the sound of their own heartbeat, the feeling of the swaddle against their cheek, the sounds or smells surrounding them in the room. Let them just BE.

- Active alert -

Active alert is all hands on deck now please. His eyes are wide open, he is looking around the room and he will be kicking around and wriggling. Time to get up and have a little gossip about stuff — and probably a feed too!

- Crying/Fussy -

Crying/Fussy is exactly what it says on the tin. Shouty, grumpy, screamy or perhaps all three in the space of one minute. Now it boils down to you to work out what he needs. With practice, you will probably be able to anticipate his needs long before this stage but for now you have to go through your check list and see if you can solve the mystery.

It usually ends up being hunger, wind, discomfort (nappy), too hot or cold or overtired. Sometimes it is none of the above which I generally refer to as the "Buggered-If-I-Know" state!

- When do growth spurts occur? -

I have always calculated the growth spurts from the baby's due date, rather than their birth date, so it may help you to stay ahead of the game if you use the same rules.

Some health professionals calculate the timing of growth spurts from the date the baby was born. I've never really agreed with this. For example, if the baby were to arrive 2 weeks early, they would not simply zoom ahead in development to catch up, would they? Conversely, if they were two weeks late, they would not go into a state of suspended development in the womb.

I have always calculated the growth spurts from the baby's due date, and it may help you stay ahead of the game if use the same rule.

Spurts typically occur at 3 weeks (although this one I find is hardly noticeable, aside from slightly increased frequency of feeds and more unsettled behaviour), 6, 9 & 12 weeks. Of course, there are more but as this book is about the first twelve weeks, then that is what I will cover here.

Growth spurts are a part of infant development. If you pop them in your phone diary with an alarm or on your kitchen calendar in big red letters, you may feel better prepared when they strike.

CHAPTER 15

WTFs, Week By Week

"Try to remind yourself that you are not going to be facing a firing line of Judging Mothers who will be checking your every move".

Week One

This is the practically vertical learning curve for both you as parents and for your new baby. Everyone will be focussed on the feeding, coping with breast feeding issues or any of the issues outlined in the Common Problems in the Early Days section.

Lots is going on as your baby adapts to life outside the womb and it's better just to go with the flow for a while. Your midwife team should give you plenty of support and guidance during these early weeks.

- How you may feel -

The comings and goings of midwives, happy visitors and relatives may leave you feeling frayed and a little under the microscope. Make time to just slink away to lie on your bed and if too many people begin to encroach on this very private time, you must be firm and express the need to be left in peace as you settle in at home

The effects of fractured sleep, or very little sleep, will start to take their toll and it is worth heeding all those irritating people who keep telling you to sleep when the baby does. It may only be half an hour here and there, but this will help you cope while your own body learns to function without your standard eight hours. The laundry and emails must wait! Prioritise.

If you are feeling a little trapped by being in the house all the time, do go out for a walk and pop the baby in the buggy. Don't overdo it on distance but do get some fresh air. I will cover getting out and about in more detail at the Three Week stage.

WEEK TWO

It may be that some of the early days problems never happened and you have breezed through the first week, but it's always better to be well informed for the road ahead.

If you had the ghost of a feeding routine forming, then it is likely to go wobbly for a while now. Don't despair. This is normal and simply not worth fighting against.

- How you may feel -

Now begins the plod. If you are part of an antenatal group, then about now you can expect your texting thread to be awash with baby comparisons and questions about what each of you is experiencing. Feeding issues, episiotomy chats, C-section recoveries and breastfeeding problems will be on the menu for a little while longer.

The message thread will gradually move into exchanges about why your baby won't settle, and they will all start looking stuff up online to further fuel their angst.

I've advised you to be wary about the sources of information on the internet, because it is probably about now that you will start dipping your toe in. Just be mindful that opinions and theories are plentiful on the surface, but reliable and researched facts need a deeper dig.

It is not unusual for partners to become more stressed and fractious with each other towards the end of Week 2. Tiredness is kicking in and, if your partner only has two weeks of paternity leave, then both of you will be feeling anxious about this.

By now your baby's poo will probably have transitioned from the dark meconium stage to the mustardy yellow shade, so the midwives will be happily ticking boxes and awarding you "best poop in class" rosettes. Take it that you are doing well with the feeding and celebrate this little milestone.

If you are still experiencing breast feeding problems (latch, sore nipples etc.) then please seek help.

Reflux, the discomfort suffered by babies due to regurgitation of stomach acids, can rear its ugly head around the end of Week Two. Even for hardened professionals, it is sometimes hard to differentiate between a baby just being a baby vs. a baby who has this problem.

Symptoms such as frequent waking, back arching, long periods of inconsolable crying, an inability to settle flat on their back and a need to be held upright for hours can all be signs of a baby suffering with silent reflux. Frustratingly, they can also be symptoms of overtiredness, overstimulation, intestinal wind or even just standard behaviour for a newborn.

Don't be too quick to hang a label as the worst-case scenario. Focus instead on ensuring that you are spacing the feeds well. There is no need to stick to rigid scheduled times, but simply make sure that you are waiting for a while from the end of one feed to the start of the next.

If, every time your baby cries, your default setting is to feed him then you may exacerbate the problem. If he wasn't actually hungry but simply telling you that he was getting tired, throwing down more food into a tum full of half-digested milk will simply make things worse. That tum needs time for the acids produced to do their job before moving the contents further into the gut for processing. Constant feeding without sensible breaks could make him more uncomfortable.

For the first six weeks or so, try to aim for an average of 3 hours between feeds. For example: if you feed him at 9am, then he could probably manage to nap from 10.15 until noon quite happily if he has taken a good feed.

If you have a bigger baby who is piling on the pounds, he may last until 12.30pm until needing another feed. Conversely, a smaller chap may want another feed at 11.30am. Either way, if he has taken a good feed between 9-10am, it is unlikely that hunger is the issue if he wakes at 10.45. That is more likely to be the end of a sleep cycle than a need for more food.

- Sleep cycles explained -

Over the past few years I've lost count of how many home visits have uncovered the same issue. Namely, not realising that babies sleep in cycles of 45 minutes.

As a result, when a baby wakes mid-nap (i.e. at the 45-minute mark), the parent presumes either a) they are hungry again or b) there is something they need. This means baby gets picked up from the cot which fully rouses them.

With a little bit of help early on, it is possible to teach a baby to join these cycles of sleep together which, in turn, means your baby will sleep for 1.5 hours rather than just 45 minutes between wake ups.

WEEK THREE

Towards the middle of the third week, your baby will be gearing up for his first growth spurt at Three Weeks old. As the first leg of the journey is a steep learning curve anyway, unsettled behaviour is part of your new normal, so you probably won't notice any subtle changes at this point other than an increased demand for feeds.

Your baby will probably pop into and out of his 3-week growth spurt without you really registering much change in his behaviour. At best, you may feel that his feeding frequency increases. As the whole experience is still very new and unfamiliar to you, it would take an expert eye to spot it come and go.

By now, if all is well with you and your baby, you will probably have been signed off by your midwives and Health Visitor.

- What changes after this growth spurt? -

Subtle little changes are noticeable, such as the baby opening their eyes a little more and having a good look around. They may lock on to stark contrasts such as a light window with a divide across it, a black picture frame against a light wall or turn to the sound of your voice when you speak.

You may find that the bouncy chair, until now a definite no-no in the baby's opinion, becomes somewhere he quite enjoys hanging out. If he is happy to remain awake happily for 10 minutes after a feed, you can pop him in it. Grab the opportunity to have a shower in peace while he entertains you on the other side of the glass.

Equally, you may find that the baby might not be quite ready for it. Wait for another few days if it is not a big hit. Instead, after a feed spend a few minutes with your baby on your lap while you chat to him or put him down on his play-mat to have a little kick about. This playtime may only be about 5-10 minutes now, but as his tolerance to stimulation increases over time, so will the length of time he can play on his mat independently. Don't rush him. He's still very little.

If he seems alert and interested in looking around a bit after a feed, you could introduce a little time on his playmat now. A little time on his back, with a few dangly toys to entertain him, and a minute or two on his tummy to help stretch out those little back muscles. Tummy time can be a little hit and miss, so let your baby lead you. If you put him down and he reacts as though you've just put him in the path of an oncoming tractor, it's probably best to leave it till next week and try again!

Baby growling is something that crops up around now. Sounding as though the baby is trying to shit out a lawnmower, he will make loud and long straining noises, often writhing around in his sleep. I first noted this happening over 22 years ago when I became aware that every baby I worked with did the same thing at around the same age.

Despite quizzing many osteopaths and doctors, nobody has yet been able to give me a definitive answer about why they do this. More often than not, the baby will actually be asleep when doing this. I have had many clients who have greeted me with a black screened mobile phone, showing me filmed footage of the noises in the night.

Now, obviously I have seen this behaviour many thousands of times, but to a new parent it can seem a little scary. The noises emanating from the crib in the dark may make you wonder if your baby is possessed by evil spirits. Some of the soundtracks I've had texted to me would certainly not be out of place in a horror movie, yet the babies, for the most part, don't seem unduly bothered.

My theory (and it is only a theory), is that you have a little person there who has been squished up inside you for many months, now gaining weight at considerable speed, so is unravelling and extending in equal measure. Perhaps this pushing and grunting is just their way of allowing their body to deal with it. It does tend to look as though they are almost re-setting their body, and as long as the baby does not seem to be distressed there seems little point in over-thinking it. The majority of the time, this phase passes within a week or two.

- Getting out of the house -

After the dust has settled and you are staggering out of the fog that was your first 3-4 weeks, your thoughts will turn to the Big Outdoors and the prospect of being able to plan a bit of a social life, weekends away or just getting out and about more.

It's likely that you have had to do the odd mad dash to the shops or to see your doctor, but the logistics involved in getting out of the house for more than an hour can feel as if you are planning a tactical raid in Churchill's War Rooms.

Once again — it's all about being prepared for battle.

You will probably have been suffering from a bit of cabin fever for a week or two, so going for stomp around the park will feel like a real treat. At first though it can seem daunting. After all, with only the barest bones of routine in place and a seemingly endless cycle of sleeping and feeding, it seems a big ask. But unless you intend to spend the rest of your days cooped up at home you have to take the plunge.

Try to remind yourself that you are not going to be facing a firing line of Judging Mothers who will be checking your every move. Far from it. Other mothers will be hurtling around with a list of chores as long as your arm, all of which have to be completed before their own little shitty time bomb in a nappy ignites for a feed again, so they are unlikely to give you a second glance.

You will need to pack a Daily Adventures Nappy Bag: a portable, temporary nursery if you like. It needs to be relatively large, even for a newborn, so that you can upgrade the contents as your baby, like a small Incredible Hulk, bursts out of outfit after outfit over the coming months.

This larger bag can be abandoned for something smaller and more practical if you are just doing a mad dash to the chemist/supermarket, in which case take the bare minimum needed such as a nappy and wipes.

For all other expeditions, you'll need to take clothing, nappies, potions, changes of clothes etc. whenever you leave the house for more than a couple of hours, so better to have it packed in advance for a quick escape.

This is a little list which you may find helpful for quick trips of 1-2 hours:

🍼 3-4 NAPPIES

🍼 2 MUSLIN CLOTHS

🍼 FORMULA FED BABIES ONLY
1-2 cartons of readymade formula (add to this number depending on how long you intend to be out on any given day).

🍼 1 FULL CHANGE OF CLOTHES FOR BABY

🍼 1 CLEAN T-SHIRT OR TOP FOR YOU
This is in case baby throws up/poos on you.

🧸 1 DUMMY

Useful for traffic jams or visits that involve injections or confined spaces, such as buses or trains.

🧸 1 PACK OF BABY WIPES IN A TRAVEL POUCH

£20-£40 cash in case you have a sudden need for a taxi/coffee/sticky bun, and you find you have forgotten your main purse!

🧸 RED BOOK

This is your baby's health record given to you by the Health Visitor. Should you ever have cause to leave the house in a hurry (e.g. baby poorly/clinic/A&E), you will always grab the bag and therefore will immediately have that information to hand.

When you are thinking of heading out for a more extended adventure (visiting friends/relatives a few miles away for example), add an extra 2-3 nappies, more ready-made milk (where relevant), perhaps 2 x outfits for the baby and an extra muslin.

If breastfeeding, I would advise at least trying to engineer the timings so that you feed the baby shortly before you leave the house. This should help secure at least a quiet couple of hours as you travel.

If giving EBM, take the required amount of milk out of the freezer and stand it in a bowl of cold water to start defrosting it about 30 mins before you plan to leave. Once it is pourable, put it into bottle/bottles, put the bottle into a thermo bag and the thermo bag into the Nappy Bag. If your baby takes only warmed milk, then you will need to ensure you are somewhere with the necessary amenities when the feed time comes.

If giving formula feeds: make up bottle/bottles according to the number of feeds you plan to do while out, put the (hot) bottles into the thermo bag and put that into the Nappy Bag. Measure out the scoops of formula into a compartmentalised pot - this is available in most baby departments - and pop that in too. As with EBM, you will need to find somewhere suitable to warm the bottles if necessary.

While guidelines stipulate that you need to add formula powder to water that has been boiled and cooled for 30 mins, if you take a bottle with relatively hot water in it in a thermo bag, this should suffice. You can cool it down after adding the powder if needs be.

- Planning the escape -

Before you wake baby up for their next feed, have your handbag and coat, house keys/car keys and phone ready inside the front door then rouse the baby. Do your first feed at home then pop baby down in the buggy, grab a coat, keys, phone, handbag and .... um .... Oh yes! ... and the baby — then head out for your adventure.

Depending on which type of buggy you have, you will also want to make sure you have the add-ons for our wonderfully unpredictable British weather.

For British Summer: A rain cover and a compact umbrella! Keep them stashed permanently underneath the bassinette in that annoying little underbelly, which serves no purpose other to transport two tins of baked beans, break nails or to tip you completely over the edge when trying to load it with an excessive amount of shopping. In the rain. While your baby is screaming blue murder because you are running late.

A muslin attached to the hood with a couple of strategically placed clothes pegs or hair clips will help reduce glare and visual stimulation. If you are in a busy street or restaurant when nap time comes around, this might help your baby drift off. If it is a particularly hot day, then make sure that you check the temperature under the hood is not getting too warm. For hotter weather you might like to buy a ventilated mesh which does the same job.

For British Autumn/Winter: Still the rain cover and the umbrella but now add in the wind proof cover for the buggy. In the damper, colder months of winter it's probably worth putting a little sheepskin underneath the mattress. Most of us think to put blankets and wind proofing on top of the baby, but when it is icy cold, there is not much insulation between your baby's back and the chilly winds blowing underneath the bassinette.

In autumn, winter and quite likely into late springtime, you will need to put a warm hat on your baby when out and about. However, you must take it off if you decide to plunge into a hot department store or shopping centre for half an hour. Also, remember to peel back a layer of blanket cover if it is really warm inside. While you are shopping your baby will be gently coming to the boil under all that cold weather gear.

Weeks Four to Six

If you are breastfeeding, you will probably find that by now you are both getting the hang of it quite well. A good supply & demand rhythm has probably begun to feel more established and you may even be expressing some feeds. That being the case, Dads/partners can help out from time to time, or you can meet a friend for lunch out, leaving your baby for a few hours with a family member.

- How you may feel -

Probably by Week Four, you will have begun to get your head around the fact that babies just don't operate to our wishes. No matter how many books you might have read to the contrary, the first few weeks will see you struggle to find a balance between your needs and those of the baby, and you may quite possibly have used up all your swearing allowance within the first week. Perhaps invest in a Swear Box and use the (massive amount of) money to go out for a meal once you mastered this whole motherhood shit.

The other amazing thing that starts to happen is that you begin to adapt to the broken sleep. This is a wholly welcome advantage of being the one with the crazy hormones. Fractured nights, unpredictable days and recovery from giving birth really take their toll on a new mum.

Mothers who, up until now, would shun the idea of an afternoon nap with a shrug, saying, "I never normally sleep in the daytime", have been herded off to bed on my watch, only to be found some 20 minutes later slumped on their beds, mobile phone in hand, drooling and snoring like a tranquilised zoo animal.

Sure, you may not have been an afternoon napper 11 months ago, but 11 months ago you hadn't produced a baby, had you?!

Grab those hormones and give them a hug and go to sleep as often as you can. You have a few more weeks to go until longer blocks of sleep are likely, so don't be a bloody martyr.

- What changes after this growth spurt? -

If you have been giving your baby a little bit of time on their tummy, you will probably see them starting to lift their head off the mat a little more as their strength increases.

Given that their head often weighs considerably more than the rest of their body to start with, this skill may take a while. If you have a baby with a bigger head, then clearly more gym time will be needed and that is where frequent tummy time becomes beneficial.

Loud noises (banging doors or dogs barking) may make them startle more, and cry as a result. But they will become more and more interactive, looking at your face and starting to make little squeaks and cooing noises.

At around the five-week mark, they will get revved up for the 6 Week Growth Spurt. Where you may have had a short period of stability following the 3 Weeker, they may become hungry more frequently again.

Don't panic! This is natural, so you simply feed a little more often until he sails past the 6-Weeker finishing line shortly before he reaches the start of Week 7. After that, he should ease back into the previous pattern without much trouble.

After six weeks, babies become much more interactive, beginning to recognise simple patterns. You may find he will gaze at your face, mapping every detail as his eyes flick around while getting to know you in better focus.

Around now, he may start to work towards his first smiles. It may take practice, so be patient with him.

Babies find eye to eye contact quite overwhelming after a short time. Just to make my point — grab your partner/mum/passing friend and just sit in silence and stare into each other's eyes for one full minute. Bet you wanted to look away before 20 seconds were up, right?

Babies can find this level of interaction quite tiring. If you get one or two smiles after a week or so, don't be surprised if you just have to make do with that. Just for now. Soon he will be beaming at you several times a day and laughing at your facial reaction to one of "those" nappy changes. You'll understand what I mean by that soon enough!

In my profession, time and time again I come across new parents who are not really aware of how little stimulation these very young babies can handle. They see them as this new little fully formed human being and assume that they feel, perceive or anticipate things much as we grown-ups do.

This is not the case. Newborns are very sensitive to over-stimulation, over-handling or other noise/activity going on around them. A high level of input, more often than not, will result in the baby reaching saturation point and, unable to cope with the "chaotic impact" on their senses, will simply have a melt-down.

This is adrenaline kicking in and is their natural coping mechanism

How many tiny babies have you witnessed launching into full cry after being passed from relative to relative for their "cuddle"? How many little ones have you seen crumple in a fit of tears and tantrums at 5pm after a frenetic and bouncy tea party? How many shrieking infants do we see being wheeled around loud, crowded, bright supermarkets?

Most of these incidents are a direct result of over-stimulation, and this is how young babies employ their "coping mechanism". They scrunch their eyes closed, they throw out their arms (Moro reflex) and they scream, Oooowah, Oooowah, Oooowah over and over again. This is their equivalent of us sticking our fingers in our ears, shutting our eyes and saying, "I can't hear you; I can't hear you".

It is the only method they can employ to distance themselves from whatever is bothering them and a way of venting the tension they feel.

Take the baby away from the source of this stress and you stand a chance of being able to calm them down and help them go off to sleep. Keep them where they are and ignore those signs, and you will have a hugely over-tired and miserable baby.

Kiss that one goodbye and let's focus on the next one.

You are now a night owl, hardcore mum with only a few scars (those scratch marks on your breasts count!) and a slight tick in your right eye. It's Week 5.5, and now you find yourself in full Warrior Pose, facing the perfect storm that is gathering momentum on the horizon.

Unlike the post-spurt period which followed the Three Weeker, where you may have found that other than a slightly more alert baby, not much changed. The Six Weeker is a much more noticeable leap.

WEEKS SIX TO NINE

At this point in time, I'd like to think that you are getting more accustomed to baby's temperament and your feeding/awake/sleep patterns are becoming much more predictable than they were at four weeks.

The postnatal expectations of life with a newborn will have taken a sharp slap in the face, and you appreciate now how hard a job it is.

You will not be having breakfast on the terrace in your White Company nightwear while your peaceful infant snoozes amongst swathes of matching white bedding upstairs. Quite honestly, if you have managed to eat something before 10am, popped on some laundry and had a shower before midday you are doing bloody well, girl.

As with most growth spurts, this next one will manifest itself with an increased frequency of feeds and … sorry but yes, another period of unsettled behaviour. If you are breastfeeding, your baby is merely sending a message to the breasts that more food is required.

By cluster feeding like this, the breasts eventually respond by producing more milk and usually bang on time for the start of the growth spurt. If he begins getting more frantic for feeds at 5.5 weeks, by the time the breasts have responded and started to increase the amount delivered, he will be on the starting line for the growth spurt. Mother Nature is dead clever, really. (Well, we'll work on the Maldives thing!)

These periods last an average of 3-5 days. Once your baby has the amount of milk he needs, he will chomp happily away at regular intervals, and you could well see him pile on a bunch of weight as well as grow in both girth and length. Once the spurt is over, he will return to his more normal self and settle down until the next growth spurt.

- What changes after this growth spurt? -

Your baby may have become much less theatrical during nappy changes or after bath times, and you are probably feeling a lot more confident in handling and comforting your tiny terrorist. Now you will start to see a much more engaged and present little person.

During the next few weeks, you may notice that burping him becomes easier. The possets become less frequent and any issues he had with passing wind are starting to improve.

He will be more likely to take a full feed and then spend 10-15 minutes having quiet playtime on his activity mat before his daytime naps, whereas previously he would have conked out fairly swiftly following a feed.

Smiles will become more regular from about 6/7 weeks onwards. You may have been lucky enough to have been given a few crooked attempts earlier than this, but they are worth the wait. That gummy little face, beaming up at you from the changing mat will melt you. It'll be better than a bunch of flowers after all the work you have put in over the past few weeks and will have you sprinting down the road to reclaim the registration form you posted to the orphanage.

Enjoy this change in your baby and start interacting with him more. You can now get more use out of the playmat. If you have bought (or been given) one, then please order in a few brightly coloured or black/white toys to add to the mix.

Neutral colours are boring at the best of times, but to a new baby who is waking up to the world, if it were weather it would be drizzle! Tango Orange and Rainforest Green may not match your Farrow & Ball "Mole's Breath" carpet or your "Stonehenge Grey" walls, but your baby will love it. And remember, it's all about him right now.

In a few months you can store the entire ugly heap up in the loft until you are mad enough to do this all over again. During playtimes you can spend some of the time engaging with him but try to also allow him space to simply bop around on his own on his playmat. Dangle the toys so that he accidentally swipes them.

The movement will keep him fascinated and distracted. He will enjoy exploring this new world of colour and vibration whilst you get a load of laundry on or have some breakfast. After all, you've probably been moaning about being time-poor for the past six weeks, so give both him and you a bit of space.

You can also now start to encourage more time on his front. This is cutely referred to as Tummy Time. There are some excellent playtime mats available which make this activity much more fun. Previous attempts at tummy time may have been greeted with grizzling or melt downs and certainly I've never found that my lot like it much until about now. Some babies just spread out like a melting choc-ice, completely non-plussed by the whole experience, but it will help him become accustomed to the position and gently strengthen his neck, abdominal and back muscles.

In proportion to his body, his head is cumbersome, so lying on his tum may have been a short-lived and frustrating exercise to date. As his core muscles grow stronger, you will find that he can hold his head up for a little longer each week.

You can roll up a towel or muslin to put under his chest which will help to lift his shoulders off the floor a little. As his shoulders are elevated, so is his head and that makes the room a helluva lot more exciting for him.

Tummy time can also be as simple an exercise as positioning him on your own tummy as you lie prone. You can then pull faces at each other while he gazes at you from close quarters.

He may start to stare at shadows on the wall, contrasting pictures perhaps, or patterns created by walking him under leafy trees in the buggy. He may begin to make odd noises or sounds — the beginnings of language!

If the first noises sound remarkably like "fuck" or "shit", you only have yourselves to blame! Introduce a Swear Tin and start saving for a trip to the Maldives. It shouldn't take long at this stage, so I'd start looking at flights now if I were you!

THE NINE WEEK GROWTH SPURT

Reflexes that were noticeable when he was born will start to disappear now. The sucking reflex fades as he can now see more clearly and find the nipple with his eyes rather than bopping his head around like a middle-aged man at a wedding disco when a Rolling Stones number comes on.

He may start to produce more varied sounds now — squeaks for pleasure, donkey-like giggles on the changing mat, chirrups and coos when waking up in his cot. One of my clients described her son as sounding like a cross between a dolphin and a goat. Not my words, hers!

He will have been hearing sounds around him for many weeks, but the introduction of music at playtimes may be a fun way to mix up the days a bit now. Nursery rhymes, classical music or even your fave tunes as you boogie around getting jobs done will keep him stimulated and entertained.

If you haven't already moved him from his Moses basket for naps, then you may find that now might be a good time to acclimatise him to his room and cot. He will become much more aware of his surrounding as his 3D eyesight develops over the next couple of months, so it's a great time to start getting him accustomed to his new Mission Control area. Quite apart from that, he must be huge by now, so before he begins to emerge from his naps with the imprint of wicker on his cheeks, set up the cot and upgrade him.

Hopefully, you will be coming out of the fog now. The first two months are behind you and you are still here. Acknowledge that fact and look how far you have come.

- What changes after this growth spurt? -

Reflexes that were noticeable when he was born will start to disappear. The sucking reflex fades as he can now see more clearly and find the nipple with his eyes rather than bopping around with his nose and mouth. He will startle less often as his environment becomes more familiar to him.

His movements become more fluid and controlled with tummy time eliciting occasional mini push-ups, lifting his head and shoulders off the floor.

THE TWELVE WEEK GROWTH SPURT

Well, you've reached the Three-Month Flag. Bloody well done!

I wonder how much you can remember about your first day at home. Why don't you go and look at that photo I told you to take on your phone as you came through the door?

I'll bet it feels like eons ago and will help to make you feel like goddam Wonder Woman for surviving this far.

As with all the preceding spurts, you will see changes both before and after the developmental jump. However, as your baby is now considerably larger than he was 11 weeks ago, the feeding frenzy that has accompanied the past few leaps is not as exaggerated this time around. He has piled on a couple of kilos or more since birth and now posturing and flexing like Mr Universe.

This growth spurt is the very hungry caterpillar becoming the butterfly, and your delicate little newborn is becoming a distant memory. OK, he may be more butterball than butterfly, and you might be able to park your bicycle in those thigh creases, and his arms may be so chubby that he can hardly bend — but he is still a butterfly.

- What changes after this growth spurt? -

"Hands! How exciting ... and they belong to me!"

This is a fun stage as your baby begins to notice parts of his body that he can control, such as hands and feet. As he gets to grips with his new "toys", he will start gradually reaching out, jerkily at first, grasping at objects hanging over him or handed to him.

Considering how intricate a piece of kit a hand is, don't expect him to be able to thread a needle in a week. It's a work in progress that has to be built — from batting toys to holding them, from squashing bits of cooked carrot into his own ear to picking them up to eat (carrots, not ears). He will start eating the contents of his nose in time but that's a whole other book.

You will see that his eyes, previously showing an independence similar to a chameleon, are now starting to work as a team more often. As a result, he will be able to focus on objects in dimension, and as his brain develops over the next week or two you may see him starting to focus on different objects. This focus turns into an obsession, as he works out how to steer those chubby little arms and hands in the right direction and capture his prey!

Concentrating on an object for more than half a minute is intense for your baby. It's the equivalent of an adult doing a task for an hour or so. Don't expect that initial interest for a waggling toy in his face to last for too long. Mix it up, move him from mat to bouncy chair, bouncy chair to cot, cot to hip as you wander around the house. If you have jobs to do and need to pop out, then a quick jaunt in the sling will be most welcome. He wants to meet and greet his public now.

Bottle (formula) fed babies weighing around 5.5kg/12lbs may well drop one of the night feeds now. Breast fed babies may still need night feeds for a little while longer. Again, they tend to do this when they are ready.

- What is actually going on in there? -

His eye muscles are growing stronger, and that enchanting boss-eyed squint that adorned many an Instagram post becomes less frequent.

He'll track objects in motion, following the arc of a toy moved across his line of sight or map you moving across a room.

He will really enjoy bright, contrasting colours, see you approaching from across a room and greet you with smiles.

Music is fun for babies at this age. They enjoy listening to a variety of tunes and voices, including environmental sounds. Have some nursery rhymes on when he is on his play mat or in his bouncy chair. Or introduce him to some heavy rock from your youth. He may love it. If he errs on the side of Barry Manilow and you guys are definitely Meatloaf fans, it may be time for a DNA test.

He will start to explore using not only his hands but his mouth as he learns about the objects that surround him. Things will be gummed and sucked as he checks out textures.

It is possible that he may be enthusiastic about a little more tummy time now. The development of all those small core muscles needs a bit of a helping hand in preparation for rolling and crawling, so make sure you include plenty of tummy-based activities. Swimming is excellent for helping to strengthen back and abdominal muscles.

WTF DOES HE DO NEXT?

Nature, in her clever way, dishes out new skills by the bucket load from now on. Your baby's eyes will be developing fast, as will his motor skills. From about 12-14 weeks onwards, you will notice that they will start using their limbs in a much more controlled way.

His legs will be all over the place, akin to a horizonal version of Riverdance. He will express excitement, happiness and frustration by doing little bursts as Lord of the Dance. Motor skills are a work in progress too, so it will take years to perfect this little work of art.

Consider the accuracy that is eventually required from a hand: from bopping a dangling toy to reaching and grabbing objects, scrunching crackly materials, feeling soft, bobbly, rough, cold and warm things as he explores his new sensory world.

This little hand has got many years ahead of it in which to learn to use a spoon, pick up a cup, use a pen and even thread a needle. It takes a long time for these skills to become established, so be patient. Take a look at the appearance of your own handwriting at 10 years of age and now and you'll see what I mean.

You may notice that your baby will study his hand and watch it intently as he moves it around. It will be dawning on him that he has control over it and can begin to reach for objects that you hold up in front of him.

While this new skill is practised, you should see that his eyes, previously slightly wayward and often crossed, will start to work as a team as the eye muscles develop and strengthen. This double whammy of development will herald the beginning of more interactive playtime with your baby and is a great time to start going to some more involving playgroups.

Rather than only getting together with your antenatal group, it is essential for your baby's social and physical development to begin mixing with other babies while encouraging them to explore their world a little more.

Pop him on his tummy and put a little free-standing mirror (a make-up mirror for example) on the floor in front of him so he can look at his reflection; put toys to each side of the mirror, just within his grasp so he can begin to reach out for them. When he begins to frown or fuss, simply move him onto his back for the remaining playtime. Each day he will build up not only his strength but confidence in this position, and when the time comes for rolling, he will not find this inverted view of his world quite as startling.

Be warned: if you lie down next to him on the floor, there is always a danger that you will grab the opportunity to fall asleep! We call that playing Sleeping Bunnies. Seize the opportunity for a quick nap, girl — he won't even notice.

When you are pottering around the nursery putting clothes away, instead of plonking him on the playmat on the floor, you can try putting him in his new bed. If it has a mobile, all the better. Oh, and I don't mean so that he can text his mates, I mean the kind of mobile with dangly toys on.

If you can find one with bright and contrasting colours so much the better. Beige is still sooo boring for a baby, no matter how Zen-like you may have felt it was when you bought it. Anyway, it's not for you; it's for him. Let him have the 60s throwback of zany lime greens, oranges and three shades of turquoise along with parts which move, zigzags and chequerboard patterns too. He'll still love it.

Cot toys that can be safely tied to the bars can be fun at this stage. Over the next few weeks, he will be discovering the use of his hands. Having something to reach out for and fiddle with will keep him occupied for long enough for you to put away the laundry.

I have always found that by getting babies accustomed to their cot environment as early as possible, it soon becomes a much more fun place for them to hang out as time goes on. The nursery will, by default, become a more frequented space, but by being in the cot for certain parts of the day, your baby will probably transition more smoothly when the time comes for him to leave your bedroom.

At this point, if your cot is still a dumping ground for clothes that were too big, unwanted gifts or things you bought and never used, then now is the time to do a spring clean.

THE BABY WILL FIT AROUND MY LIFE!
(YEAH, RIGHT.)

By the time your child reaches the age of one, I'm presuming that you aim to have a getting up time, a breakfast time, a lunch time and a bath to bedtime. Then a routine huh? How do you think you get there if you don't start building the habits at some point? It doesn't just *happen*.

Hundreds of desperately tired parents use tricks to coax, cajole or bribe a very overtired and irritable small person JUST. TO. GET. SOME. BLOODY. SLEEP!

During the past 24 years I have spent weeks re-setting habits in 5/6-month old babies. Their weary parents had tried their best to get the baby to nod off by using some or all of the following methods:

- Parking the baby next to a noisy tumble drier.
- Driving back and forth up and down the A3 until the car ran out of petrol — at 3am. Sitting in the car with the engine running whilst baby slept in the back seat. 3 hourly tag-teamed shifts bobbing baby up and down on a Swiss Ball. Sleeping beside the baby with a little finger inserted in baby's mouth. Hot water bottle on mattress prior to putting sleeping baby down.
- Standing over the cot whilst running a hair drier.
- Gizmos which re-create the sounds of the womb.
- Total black-out using tin foil on windows.
- Apps of white noise placed in the cot.
- Lavender spray on the mattress.

- Heartbeat sounds Teddy Bear
- Radio set to static noise
- Enya playing on loop (kill me now!)
- White Noise sheep
- Musical mobiles
- Vibrating chairs
- Dummies
- Rocking
- Wine
- G

  i

  n
- Or, teach your baby how to settle without your input.

In each of the above cases, the parents had reached breaking point just before they contacted me, accepting that not one of these habits was practical or sustainable in the long term. They were exhausted and miserable, as were the babies.

These parents clawed their way towards clarity, predictability and some semblance of order, like Scrat in the Ice Age movies, desperate to teach their baby to settle by themselves, yet not really understanding how a baby's sleep cycles work. (In case you haven't seen Ice Age — and you really should —Scrat is the prehistoric sabre-toothed squirrel who spends his days in endless pursuit of a seemingly unreachable acorn; bloodshot eyed, maniacal, with a permanent eye tick, teetering on the brink of losing his shit completely as he seeks his holy grail).

Even haters of routines, attachment parenting method fans

and baby-led families must succumb to *some* form of structure eventually, mustn't they? They will wake their children in the morning and make pitstops for teeth brushing, face washing, meeting certain hygiene standards prior to starting their day. They will have breakfast and continue rolling through the day, pausing for lunch and supper. Parents will have bedtime pinned onto their route map, won't they?

We all know that most children will not dictate when they will sit down for breakfast, where and when they will take their supper or at what time they will go to bed. Parents organize that for them, don't they? That's what the whole "being a parent" thing is about. So, you see, it is inevitable that before long, you too will have to have some kind of building blocks in place and an end goal to work towards.

- Spaced feeding (no illegal narcotics needed) -

You will have probably had it drummed into you by now that babies feed "roughly every 2-4 hours". That can sound like a very small window and leave you wondering when on earth you are supposed to sleep, eat or shower.

How often, and indeed how much you have to feed your newborn boils down to how often they need it. A baby delivered 3 weeks before term may need to feed little and often until he reaches a healthier weight, perhaps as much as every 1.5-2 hours. Whereas a full-term bouncing 4kg baby may give you an easier ride, only needing filling up every 3.5-4 hours.

Many of my clients have spent a few days in hospital where they have been instructed by midwives to "keep the baby on that breast as long as he wants to be there".

Now, in my experience, most babies would still be there next Christmas if they were simply left on board. It is warm, cosy and super-comforting to fall asleep whilst feeding, but this is not sustainable in the longer term and certainly precludes the mother from doing anything other than spending the day rooted to the sofa. If that floats your boat, then off you trot and I'll see you next Christmas, but if you want structure and to shower, eat, sleep and see your friends again then read on.

It seems a better idea all round to encourage your baby to take a full, nourishing feed in one hit rather than being drip-fed for hours on end. So, I suggest that you get yourself comfy, have your favourite TV series on in the background and snuggle down with your baby for the next hour. By feeding in this way, you capitalise on the time available to satiate him and you make sure that he does not get overtired by being awake for too long.

With the full hour at his disposal (which includes time for winding, nappy changing and general faffing about, as they do), you can reckon that by the time the hour is up you have a full and happy chap in your lap. This applies to both breast- and bottle-fed babies by the way. Allow an hour and you can be pretty sure that your baby will have had a stonking good feed.

Once the feed is over, you can then enjoy some cuddle time, or simply allow him a little space to have a kick about on his playmat, in his bouncy chair or in his cot. When he begins to get fractious (usually about 10 minutes or so after the end of the feed), it is time to pop him down for a nap so that he can rest and digest for a while.

By starting to space feeds in this way, your baby will develop healthy eating habits rather than random snacking day and night. If you want any kind of structure to develop, this is a nice gentle way of starting it off.

This is referred to as the Eat — Awake — Sleep cycle.

These are the feed slots (roughly speaking):

7am	=	First Feed of the Day (which later becomes breakfast time)
10am	=	Mid-Morning Feed (this becomes lunch time)
1-2pm	=	Afternoon feed
5pm	=	Evening Split Feed (will become supper)
6pm	=	Bedtime Feed
10pm	=	Referred to as the Dream Feed
2-4am	=	The Middle of the Night Feed

STARTING A ROUTINE

You have survived this far, and you can probably look back over your shoulder to once again acknowledge, with a degree of pride, how far you have come, and you have survived.

Unpredictable and capricious, babies certainly don't conform to an adult's idea of a structured day. You will have begun to accept that babies cannot be squashed into an inflexible pattern to suit you, but the good news is that from about now you can start to build on the habits you already have in place and begin forming a routine.

By the time your baby reaches weaning age you will want to have some real structure to your days. Whether you live your life as if following a timetable or have a more relaxed approach to parenting, sooner or later you will need to have the bones of a routine in place.

Wake up and wash followed by breakfast and then out to some activity or other. Home in time for lunch and a nap before some more baby-shenanigans in the late afternoon. After lunch, perhaps playdates or park visits depending on the weather and home in time for some quiet time, supper, bath and bedtime.

If you have followed the book this far without actually putting any of the suggestions in place, then it may take a little longer to establish some kind of pattern, but perhaps give it a go now.

For those of you who have been building on habits chapter by chapter, I will assume you are at about Week 8 now and can slowly plod along beside me as we review your current status.

Breast fed babies will, by this stage, be bopping along, feeding 3.5-4 hourly by day and hopefully giving you one block of 4.5-5 hours overnight, perhaps surfacing for a Dream Feed around 10/.30pm and another somewhere between 2.30-4am.

Formula fed babies may well be punching out at 10.30pm and not waking again until 4am regularly. Either way, here is a suggested pattern for your daytime routine when your baby is eight weeks or older. If your timings don't quite match up with these then grab a pencil and alter them slightly so they feel more comfortable for you. This is not a hard and fast schedule; it is a **guide.**

A suggested pattern at around 8 weeks old

7am

First feed of the day. Followed by some kickabout time on the play mat

8.15-8.30am

Morning nap time. Watch out for the sleepy signs, and when you see that he is getting tired, take him away from the daytime place, swaddle him and give him a cuddle before placing him in his cot. Ideally, you want to allow him to settle himself down to sleep without you having to do that for him. If he is fussing, return to him and try again. This gives both you and the baby reassurance that all is well.

You will know him better by now, so will be feeling more confident in reading his cues.

10.15am

Top & tailing time: A nap of about 1.5+ is a good one, so if he has not already woken, then wake him now. You need to make sure he is not napping too long during the day, or he may want to party all night. Do a nappy change and a Top & Tail wash.

10.30am

Mid-morning feed. More playtime. Mix it up a little. He may become jaded with the playmat if he's plonked down there every morning.

You Tube is still a great place to look up ideas. Search for "Games to play with an 8-week-old baby".

11.30/11.45am

Down for a lunchtime nap. This is often a nap which is much longer than the morning and late afternoon slots, and usually remains in place until your child is well into toddlerhood. I'd aim for no longer than 2-2.5 hours.

2pm

Wake up time. If you let him sleep too long here, he may be a bit tricky to settle at bedtime.

If he is ravenous, then give him half a feed and then do a nappy change halfway through; otherwise you can do once he has had a nice stretch and woken up a bit.

2.15pm

Afternoon feed

3.30/4pm

Afternoon nap. Not much more than an hour. This is the last daytime nap. Babies are notoriously grumpy at this end of the day, so if he is not thrilled at being in the house, get out for a walk. It's just a sign that he is tiring and heading towards what is known as the Witching Hours.

5pm

Evening split feed. I've found that a few minutes of something like Baby Mozart's Music Festival (you can find it on YouTube) can be a nice little distraction and very calming for a baby at this point. It also buys you time to get the bath ready, clothes laid out for bedtime and any fluffing around in the nursery out of the way. If you don't have a TV or laptop on which to play it, then just some nice soothing music while he has a kickabout in his cot will be fine. This helps him associate his cot and nursery with sleep time.

5.45pm

Bath time

6.00pm

Bedtime feed. Take your time with this to help him feel nice and dozy.

6.45pm

Time to relax. By now he should be full of food, smelling lovely after his bath and nicely dopey. Settle him down, say goodnight and head down to the fridge for a glass of wine!

Working parent: please appreciate that you have been in the office all day, talking to grown-ups and not one of them have pooed on you or prevented you from having a hot cup of coffee. This is really not the time to bound through the door and start whizzing around doing Superman games with your Tiny Small.

It is a calm and gentle road to bed, so no matter how unjust you feel that is when you haven't played with them all day, your baby's needs are more important. This should be a sleep-inducing time. If you change the energy in the house, your baby will probably keep you all up until gone midnight. You really don't want that, and neither does whoever has been with them since 7am.

If you poke that hornet's nest, I hereby relinquish all responsibility for what may happen next, and your partner will probably pack their bags and leave!

- 8 weeks overnight plan -

10.30/11pm
Dream feed

2-4am
Middle of the night feed. My advice (which you can take or ignore) is to set an alarm for 3am. If you want to keep some control over the start of day slot, then for now I find it better keep a handle on the night time routine.

If he were to sleep past 3am, then he will be less likely to take a full feed at 7am and your day starts off on the wrong foot. If this happens, don't worry — just adjust your timings throughout the day so that you land on the 5pm — 7pm slot at approximately the right time.

You may be hearing other members of your baby group discussing night feeding patterns, and many of them may claim to have babies who are sleeping "through the night". Before you begin wondering what you are doing wrong — help yourself to a big pinch of salt and listen up.

Each mother will have a different definition of TTN (Through The Night), and this can vary enormously. To some, who perhaps have been feeding 2-3 hourly for weeks on end, a stretch of 4 hours qualifies. To others it means putting their fed baby down at midnight and not hearing from them again until 6am.

To me, it is when the baby has regularly settled to a sleep of 8 hours following the Dreamfeed until 6-7am. In this case, the baby has a feed around bathtime/bedtime, another one at around 10-11pm and then sleeps through until morning,

I have been knocking around in this business for long enough to have heard many tall tales when it comes to Through the Night sleeping.

I've even witnessed an ex-client (on Baby No. 2 with me at the time) boasting about how Baby No. 1 slept through from 7pm-7am at the age of four weeks!

IT. NEVER. HAPPENED! At that time, the baby was sleeping in my room anyway, and in all my years of doing live-in bookings, I rarely saw a baby sleep for 9-10 hours at a stretch before 8 weeks of age!

Babies generally feed once or twice in the night and start dropping them at around the three-month mark.

Of course, you may get the occasional night where a baby will bang out a five or six hour stretch which is great. And from time to time one of my clients will report back that their baby has nailed a 12-hour night at 10 weeks old; but a run from 11pm — 7am as a regular thing? I'd respectfully recommend that you expect 12-14 weeks being more realistic.

The bottom line is that babies tend to drop night feeds when they are ready. If you are having to continually wake your baby for feeds overnight just to stick to timings, then pick a Friday night (so you can lie in on Saturday) and just leave them be — see what happens! They may surprise you by sleeping much longer than you expected.

Breast fed babies have a tendency to need feeding overnight for longer than those on formula milk. This is why so many less scrupulous overnight maternity nurses promote the use of occasional formula feeds at the Dream Feed — it makes for a much easier night.

If that works and you'd welcome the sleep, then high five!

A SUGGESTED PATTERN FROM 12 WEEKS OLD

7am
First feed of the day. Top & Tailing: Followed by some kickabout time on the play mat.

9am
Morning nap. A nap of around 45 mins to 1hr. Babies at this age will often just conk out in their bouncy chair or on the playmat, and if that is the case, that is fine. He's happy, so don't worry about it.

10.00am
Try not to let him sleep past 10am. You need to make sure he is not napping too long during the day, or he may want to party all night.

10.15am

Mid-morning feed. More playtime. Mix it up a little. This could be a good time to seek out Happy Clappy Classes as mentioned in the previous pages.

11.45/12 noon

Down for a lunchtime nap. Most babies can manage a good long nap around lunchtime, but if your baby only wants to have 1-1.5hrs and is happy after that amount of time, then that is fine. You may need to feed them a little earlier than 2.30pm if that is the case — and as a result they may nap earlier than 4pm. But still try to stick to not letting them go past 5pm.

2.00pm

Feed time

4pm

Short afternoon nap. Not much more than an hour. If you let him sleep too long here, he may be a bit tricky at bedtime.

5.15pm

Evening split feed. If Baby Mozart is his thing now, then you can explore other options in the same series, or you may just go a bit mad. You could also do a story here. They become a hugely important part of a) a child's memories and b) a good way of winding them down. I loved my mother reading me Yurtle the Turtle, Sam & The Firefly and all the Little Grey Rabbit series. I have them on the shelf in my office!

6pm
Bath time

6.30pm
Bedtime feed

7pm
Settle down time. Say goodnight and head down to the fridge ...
you know where the wine is by now!

- 12 weeks overnight plan -

11pm
Dream feed. If, when you rouse him for the feed around 2-4am he
is super sleepy and not really interested, you can try to encourage
him to go longer, or even drop that feed altogether.

TIME TO PARTAY!

My past clients have always been a little nervous about dropping a night feed. On the one hand, they are inches away from
getting big blocks of sleep for the first time for weeks, but on the
other they are scared that messing with any semblance of a routine
will have a bad outcome.

Once babies no longer really need night feeds, it can be all too
easy to slip into one last bad habit. Feeding the baby just because
they wake in the night.

By now, you have a baby who is on the threshold of a whole

new developmental leap; a much more savvy and aware baby.

If every time I woke up in the night Bradley Cooper popped into my room with a box of Lindt Choccies, you can bet your ass that I would wake on the hour, every hour.

If you want to drop the night feeds, it's important to move forward not back. Re-introducing the idea that he needs to have a little snack to go back to sleep may ignite the Partay Animal in him! If you know that your baby is taking plenty during the day, and yet only taking the smallest of top ups in the night, then perhaps try offering an alternative method of re-settling.

He has been used to waking in the night for three months, so his body clock just needs to be gently shown how to knit his sleep cycles together, resulting in lovely long sleep until morning, without your having to feed him back to sleep.

Of course, if he does still take a good amount of milk at that night waking, then it is not quite time. Try again in a week or two.

SWADDLE TO SLEEPING BAG TRANSITION

Some of you reading this may never have swaddled, so you can skip this bit because your littles are probably strutting their stuff in a sleeping bag and rolling around their cots like a starfish in a tumble drier.

For those of you who have littles who still enjoy the familiarity of the swaddle, it is at this point in their journey that I would gently begin encouraging them to spread their little arms and learn to sleep with limbs akimbo.

My advice is to observe your baby over a few days on the play mat as he gets to grips with the use of his arm/hand coordination. Babies will often find their thumb, a finger or even a fist now, and it might become their way of self-soothing.

Once he can reach out and grab toys on the play mat/activity arch, you can experiment at nap times during the day by leaving out the one arm. Generally, I have found that it is better to release the arm that he seems to use the most to start with. Do this during his daytime naps for about 2-4 days, returning to full swaddle overnight perhaps.

When you pop him down for his daytime naps with one arm out, make sure that there are some toys tied to the bars of the cot that he can reach out to play with. He will be excited to explore things that he can fiddle with, so a suitably placed Very Hungry Caterpillar toy, crinkly-winged butterfly (the colourful Lamaze range) or rag-books are perfect for this stage.

When he seems to have the hang of one arm out, then you can do a simple cross body swaddle, releasing the other arm for day naps. At this point, you can introduce something for him to cuddle up to. Many babies now like to have a comforter of some description. Those little soft cloths with an animal head in the corner, for example, or a muslin cloth tied in a knot are ideal. Once he seems settled for naps with both arms out by day, you can simply transfer him to his sleeping bag for all periods of sleep.

Your baby's routine will change a little now. The nap in the morning will probably shorten to around 30-45 minutes around 9am. The lovely long lunchtime nap should stay in place well into toddlerhood if you are lucky and the late afternoon nap can remain in place as long as baby is still going off to sleep nicely at around 7pm.

Structured activity sessions (such as Monkey Music, Hart-beeps and Baby Gym) come into their own now. If you don't live in London, then jump onto your nearest Facebook Mum group and seek out classes suitable for your baby's age bracket. Most franchises offer a free session for you to attend as a taster. If there is nothing nearby, the perhaps get together with a group of mums, do a bit of surfing on YouTube for ideas and get your own activity session organised.

Over the next three months, your baby will develop fast. His head shape will change from about 12 weeks old, and you will observe the rounded baby shape disappearing and the child emerging.

You have reached the finish line of The First 12 Weeks with a Newborn.

Look back at how far you have come. Acknowledge that it was hard, but you did it. Promise yourself (and me) that you will be a realist and let other mums know the ups and downs of life with a newborn. Tell them that they will have great days when they'll feel on top of the world, but that they will have days when they will want to sit in the car with a box of chocolates and cry.

Tell them that each phase won't last forever and that you are always happy to help out by offering a shoulder to cry on, an ear to bend and a pot of tea to share.

I have been working with parents and their new babies for nigh on 25 years. The picture perfect images of life as a new mother as frequently portrayed on social media present a very skewed view to that which you will encounter.

I hope that this book will help you get through your first 12 weeks with a clearer, more truthful version and that that, in turn, will make it so much less stressful.

Most of all, I wish you and your little people health, love and laughter in abundance.

Wisdom can be shared.

Parenthood must be lived.

THE AFTERWORD

You may have chosen to read this book from cover to cover during the last few weeks of your pregnancy. I do hope so, because it will serve to arm you with some good tips and dispel a few myths.

If you are lying in bed looking down at the bump on the landscape, that little sleep thief who is waiting to crash into your lives, I dearly hope that you will have found some sanity and comfort in the preceding pages.

I appreciate that my approach may not be for everyone and you too will have your critics now that you are a mother. Stand firm and strong by your choices. If they work for you and your little one, that is all that matters.

Thank you for reading my book and I hope your bump brings you challenges that you can overcome, milestones that you can celebrate, tears that you can mop up over a glass of wine and, above all, a sense of pride and achievement that will lift you to the moon.

You've got this!

Printed in Great Britain
by Amazon